As one of the world's longest established
and best-known travel brands,
Cook are the experts in travel.

years our
he secrets
the world,
a wealth of
for travel.

ook as your
our next trip
and benefit from our unique heritage.

Thomas Cook **pocket** guides

FLORENCE

Your travelling companion since 1873

Thomas
Cook

Written by Pat Levy

Published by Thomas Cook Publishing
A division of Thomas Cook Tour Operations Limited
Company registration no. 3772199 England
The Thomas Cook Business Park, Unit 9, Coningsby Road,
Peterborough PE3 8SB, United Kingdom
Email: books@thomascook.com, Tel: +44 (0) 1733 416477
www.thomascookpublishing.com

Produced by Cambridge Publishing Management Limited
Burr Elm Court, Main Street, Caldecote CB23 7NU
www.cambridgepm.co.uk

ISBN: 978-1-84848-411-5

© 2006, 2008 Thomas Cook Publishing
This third edition © 2011 Thomas Cook Publishing
Text © Thomas Cook Publishing
Maps © Thomas Cook Publishing/PCGraphics (UK) Limited
Transport map © Communicarta Limited

Series Editor: Karen Beaulah
Production/DTP: Steven Collins

Printed and bound in Spain by GraphyCems

Cover photography © Photononstop/Superstock

CONTENTS

SYMBOLS KEY

The following symbols are used throughout this book:

ⓐ address 🕿 telephone 🖷 fax 🅦 website address ⓔ email
🕔 opening times Ⓝ public transport connections ❶ important

The following symbols are used on the maps:

🅸	information office	🚌	bus station
✈	airport	🚆	railway station
✚	hospital	✝	cathedral
🛡	police station	◼	point of interest
❶	numbers denote featured cafés & restaurants		

Hotels and restaurants are graded by approximate price as follows:
£ budget price **££** mid-range price **£££** expensive

▶ *The façade of the Duomo*

INTRODUCING
Florence

Introduction

At times the city of Florence seems trapped in a time bubble.
Get up high and look out over the city – you'll see a vista of ancient
rooftops, the magnificent Duomo at its heart and the Arno River
snaking gracefully away into the distance. What you see now is not

◕ *The age-old charm of Florentine* palazzi

so different from the Florence in which great artists such as Botticelli, Michelangelo and Donatello created their masterpieces, in which philosophers debated, and wealthy families and colourful personalities vied with each other for power and influence.

At other times you'll realise that Florence is a modern, thriving city. Go down into the centre and you'll find, tucked into the base of medieval buildings, Internet shops, trendy cafés, designer outlets and attractive hotels. Shiny cars and tourist buses now grind their way through streets intended for carts and horses.

Art lovers and tourists have been flocking to Florence for centuries. There is a reason for this – an abundance of spectacular art and culture. Some of it is protected in huge, popular museums, but much of it you can see simply on street corners and in calm piazzas. Keep your eyes open as you wander around the city in order to appreciate what it really has to offer.

Food, too, is an art form in the city. Many restaurants, even those that gain their main income from tourists, produce some real culinary delights. Delicatessens fill the streets with the smell of freshly baked bread and tempting cakes. *Gelaterie* sell home-made ice cream and chocolate shops fabricate ornate chocolate replicas of Davids and Duomos.

A shopper's paradise and a hotspot for fashion lovers, Florence boasts small boutiques offering fabulous clothes and leather goods by young Italian designers. Treat yourself and have a suit or a pair of shoes made to your own design.

If you need a break from this feast of the senses, you can relax in the beautiful ornamental gardens of Giardino di Bóboli. Or head up high to Piazzale Michelangelo, to gaze down at the time bubble before plunging back into the world of great masters, exquisite shops and culinary treats.

When to go

Extremes of weather are normal in Florence and the difference between high and low season is marked. Winter can be cold and wet but there are also fewer tourists. Hotels tend to be cheaper, queues are shorter and the restaurants may serve more unusual, traditional Tuscan cuisine. Spring is warm and Florence's peak tourist time. Temperatures reach sweltering levels in August and many locals take off on holiday. This marks a second low season, when you can often find good deals at hotels.

SEASONS & CLIMATE

From November to March, temperatures range between –1°C and 15°C (30–59°F). In spring temperatures begin to rise over 20°C (68°F), bringing increased rainfall and humidity. Summer is extremely hot, while autumn brings glorious colours to the countryside and very high humidity in town.

ANNUAL EVENTS

February

Carnevale Fiorentino (Florentine Carnival) Colourful processions and confetti-throwing in the ten days before Lent.

Vintage Selection Vintage clothes, accessories and household objects. Also held in July. ⓐ Stazione Leopolda ⓣ 055 212 622 ⓦ www.stazione-leopolda.com

March & April

Taste Over 130 exhibitors at this international food fair.
ⓐ Stazione Leopolda ⓣ 055 36931 ⓦ www.pittimmagine.com

Scoppio del Carro (Explosion of the Cart) A carriage loaded with fireworks is drawn to the Duomo by white oxen and ignited by a dove-shaped rocket. ⓐ Piazza del Duomo ⓣ 055 261 6051 ⓛ Easter Sunday

May
Artigianato & Palazzo (Handicraft Exhibition & Market) Artisans exhibit their creations in a beautiful 17th-century garden. ⓐ Giardino Palazzo Corsini sul Prato ⓣ 055 265 4589 ⓦ www.artigianatoepalazzo.it
Fabbrica Europa Popular festival of music and dance. ⓐ Stazione Leopolda ⓣ 055 248 0515 ⓦ www.ffeac.org

▲ *Scoppio del Carro draws the crowds*

Maggio Musicale Fiorentino Performing arts festival based in the Teatro del Maggio in Corso Italia, but with occasional events in other venues. 🕿 055 277 9350 🌐 www.maggiofiorentino.com

Terra Futura (Future Earth) Learn about the environment and the future of our planet. 🏛 Fortezza da Basso 🕿 055 49721 🌐 www.terrafutura.it

June

Festa del Grillo (Festival of the Cricket) For luck in love, buy a cricket and release it from its tiny cage on the first Sunday after Ascension. 🏛 Parco delle Cascine

Calcio in Costume This elaborate blend of rugby and wrestling stems from a 1530 match, when starving locals under siege staged a game to show their contempt for the imperial army of Pope Clement VII. 🏛 Piazza Santa Croce 🌐 www.calciostorico.it 🕘 24 June & two other days near to this date; fireworks at 22.00

September & October

ArteFirenze Modern art fair encompassing styles from Surrealist to pop. 🏛 Fortezza da Basso 🕿 055 49721 🌐 www.firenzefiera.it

Festa della Rificolona (Paper Lantern Festival) Procession of children carrying papier mâché lanterns, followed by floats and street parties. 🕿 055 290 832 (tourist office) 🌐 www.firenzeturismo.it

Biennale dell'Antiquariato The oldest biennial antiques fair in Italy. Next fair 2011. 🏛 Palazzo Corsini 🕿 055 282 635 🌐 www.mostraantiquariato.it

November & December

Florence Marathon 🕿 055 552 2957 🌐 www.firenzemarathon.it

Festival dei Popoli (People's Film Festival) International film and documentary festival at various locations around the city. 🕿 055 244 778 🌐 www.festivaldeipopoli.org

Mostra Mercato del Tartufo Bianco (White Truffle Festival) San Lorenzo's famed annual truffle festival. **ⓐ** Villa Pecori Giraldi, Borgo San Lorenzo **ⓣ** 055 849 661 **ⓦ** www.comune.borgo-san-lorenzo.fi.it
Mercato di Natale (Christmas Market) Pick up local crafts or enjoy the entertainment. **ⓐ** Stazione Leopolda **ⓣ** 055 895 3651 **ⓦ** www.florencenoel.it

---

PUBLIC HOLIDAYS
Capodanno (New Year's Day) 1 Jan
La Befana (Epiphany) 6 Jan
Pasqua & Lunedì di Pasqua (Easter Sunday & Monday)
8–9 Apr 2012, 31 Mar–1 Apr 2013
Festa della Liberazione (Liberation Day) 25 Apr
Festa del Lavoro (Labour Day) 1 May
Festa della Repubblica (Anniversary of the Republic) 2 June
Festa di San Giovanni (Feast of St John the Baptist) 24 June
(Province of Florence only)
Ferragosto (Feast of the Assumption) 15 Aug
Tutti Santi (All Saints' Day) 1 Nov
Festa dell'Immacolata (Feast of the Immaculate Conception) 8 Dec
Natale (Christmas) 25 Dec
Santo Stefano (Boxing Day) 26 Dec

During public holidays most banks and shops are shut but restaurants and cafés usually remain open. Florentines usually take their holidays in July and August, so be prepared for more shops and businesses to be closed during these months.

Designer outlets

Shopping in Florence's city centre is charming. The shops are tiny and inviting and you can often find unique handmade items or clothes. However, this is not the main reason the city has become a top shopping destination. Fashionistas flock to Florence for its unbelievable range of designer outlets, where you can pick up designer labels at bargain prices. A serious outlet shopping trip in Florence requires as much dedication and persistence as a museum or church tour, but you may walk away with a genuine Prada handbag for 100 euros – the deal of the century.

All outlets are in industrial areas and fairly difficult to find, with no public transport – an intentional choice by each fashion house to ensure that cut-price stock is not too readily available. Be sure to take a detailed map and a good navigator, or easier still a taxi. Try this pick of the best:

Space/I Pellettieri This Prada outlet also stocks Miu Miu, Helmut Lang and Jil Sander. Arrive early as queues are usual by midday. Grab a numbered ticket from the dispenser by the door in order to get in. ⓐ Località Levanella, Montevarchi ⓣ 055 978 9481 ⓛ 09.30–19.00 Mon–Sat, 10.30–18.30 Sun

The Mall Outlets for big names including Gucci, Burberry, Stella McCartney, La Perla, Armani and Yves Saint Laurent. Stop at the café next to Bottega Veneta if you need a breather. ⓐ Via Europa 8, Leccio Reggello ⓣ 055 865 7775 ⓦ www.themall.it ⓛ 10.00–19.00 daily

Fendi ⓐ Via Pian dell'Isola 66/33, Rignano sull'Arno ⓣ 055 834 981 ⓛ 09.30–18.30 Mon–Sat, 14.30–18.30 Sun

Dolce & Gabbana ⓐ Località S Maria Maddalena 49, Pian dell'Isola, Incisa in Val d'Arno ⓣ 055 833 1300 ⓛ 10.00–19.30 Mon–Sat, 10.00–19.00 Sun

If the outlets above have merely whetted your appetite, stop by a bookshop to pick up a copy of *Lo Scoprioccasioni* by Theodora Van Meurs, or visit Ⓦ www.scoprioccasioni.it. This little guide lists all the major designer outlets in Italy in both English and Italian.

🔺 *There's plenty to choose from when shopping in the city centre*

History

Like many cities in Italy, Florence started as a Roman settlement in 59 BC. After five centuries of prosperity and growth it was seized by the Goths, who were rampaging across the now dissolute Roman empire. A rapid succession of Byzantines, more Goths, Lombards and then Franks, followed, and Florence became a small fiefdom ruled over by local, bickering warlords.

Medieval Florence emerged from this economically debilitating period around the 11th century and in 1115 it and its Tuscan neighbours became independent city-states. For a couple of centuries the new and prosperous trade guilds fought with the old nobility for control of Florence. By the 13th century, the dispute was settled – the trade guilds were in charge of the Florentine republic and the economy was doing well. Then came the really big moment in Florentine history – the Renaissance, or 'Re-birth' of culture in the widest sense.

As the 15th century began, Florence was one of the biggest and wealthiest cities in Europe. The dominant Medici family, in an effort directed partly at the Almighty and partly at power and publicity, started building churches and commissioning works of art. Renaissance superstars Botticelli, Michelangelo and Donatello created masterpieces in their workshops, alongside other more everyday objects such as tea trays, headboards and wedding baskets. Botticelli's *La Primavera* started off life as a headboard for a Medici bed.

Humanist thinkers revived ancient Greek and Roman texts and the Church experienced its own Renaissance with the founding of new orders. Science flourished. Tragically, this all came to an abrupt halt with the death of Lorenzo de Medici and with the reactionary ideas of Savonarola, who burnt paintings and manuscripts in a gigantic and historic Bonfire of the Vanities in 1497. Artists and thinkers decamped to Rome, the economy went into decline and Florence shrank into a backwater for a few centuries.

In 1864 the various Italian states were unified with Florence, controversially, as their capital. Another cultural Renaissance began – not as intense as the last one – and this was the period when the city gained its parks and ring roads. In 1870, Rome replaced Florence as Italy's capital, but Florence remained a major destination for Victorian travellers and art lovers.

The next major impact on the city was World War II. Retreating German forces bombed Florence's bridges, thankfully sparing Ponte Vecchio, but that was the worst of the damage. Compared to the rest of Europe, Florence escaped relatively unscathed.

Major floods in 1966 damaged many of the city's oldest and most precious works of art as well as leaving countless families homeless. The disaster had a silver lining: salvaging and repairing the damaged artworks led to the development of sophisticated restoration techniques that are now being used to repair paintings and statues all over the world.

Apart from a shock Mafia bomb attack in 1993 which killed five people, Florence's recent history has been one of steady growth, despite the threat of international terrorism and the global recession. This, of course, has its negative side too, and the question of how to protect the city from the hand that feeds it remains open to debate. Florence's other major ongoing problem is to do with traffic and pollution. Energetic young mayor Matteo Renzi has provided fresh initiatives to combat this and other issues, including the complete closure of the historic Piazza del Duomo to all traffic.

Lifestyle

It would be easy to assume from time spent around the major sights that Florence is little more than a tourist draw, trading on the genius of former times. But the people of Florence live quite private and passionate lives.

The Florentine lifestyle is adapted to the weather, which in summer is unbearably hot around midday. To make the most of your visit it is a good idea to do as the locals do. Start early in the morning with a brief breakfast, pause for the odd espresso then take a long lunch in the middle of the day. Lunch is a social occasion – no ready-made sandwich from a snack bar – and many shops and businesses shut for two or more hours to make the most of it. Every Florentine has a favourite restaurant which they gladly share with those tourists who have ventured away from the big *piazze*, or squares.

With the long lunch comes late opening. Shops and businesses start to reopen around 15.00 and the streets get more and more lively as families come out to shop, eat or stroll around the city. Popular places to walk are along the river, around Parco delle Cascine or through the gardens leading up to Piazzale Michelangelo.

Dinner is generally eaten fairly late in Florence and meals are relaxed and drawn out. After work or at the weekend young Florentines like to go to a bar, starting off with an *aperitivo* at their favourite café-bar and going on to one of the city's clubs. Sunday is a day for families and the parks fill up with family picnics and football teams.

In summer, when the heat and crowds can be oppressive, many shops and businesses close down for a fortnight and locals go off to the seaside for a break.

A modern lifestyle doesn't always sit too comfortably in this ancient city. Florence is overwhelmed at times by both traffic and schemes for traffic improvement, such as the new high-speed railway station. Improvements to the airport and the first phase of the much-contested tramline are now complete, but it all takes time. In summer the pollution can become so bad that traffic is banned from the city centre and it is then, and sometimes on Sunday mornings throughout the year, that you get a sense of what Florence was once like – peaceful narrow streets, hidden gardens and beautifully decorated neighbourhoods.

⬥ Scooters may be the easiest way to get around, but parking is a problem

Culture

As long ago as the medieval period, powerful Florentines were commissioning works of art ranging from cathedrals to furniture for their luxurious *palazzi* (while the Italian *palazzo* sounds like 'palace' in English, the word can be used to imply anything from a mansion to a royal home). Art became an industry, with master painters and sculptors managing workshops of apprentices. For an example of this medieval style, look at the simple images backed by gold leaf by artists such as Cimabue.

Change came with artists such as Giotto (1267–1337), who began to paint expressions on the faces of figures set in naturalistic landscapes. Ghiberti and his apprentice Donatello (1386–1466) created naturalistic designs in bronze, for example those on the doors of the Baptistery (see pages 82–5). Donatello went on to create lifelike statues standing in natural poses, including the bronze *David* and the *St George*, now in the Bargello Museum (see page 65).

The young Masaccio (1401–28) changed the direction of Renaissance painting by introducing scientific perspective and stronger realism into his works. His frescoes – such as those in the church of Santa Maria del Carmine (see page 106) – are the first examples of humanism in art and their influence was immense. Just a few years later in 1439, the Tuscan monk Fra Angelico shocked the art world with his altarpiece at the newly built monastery of San Marco (see page 92), which depicts saints as real figures standing and chatting naturally around the Madonna and her infant Jesus.

Artists subsequently started adding their employers' faces, sitting rooms and palaces to paintings. You will see members of the Medici family, who commissioned much of the art, all over the city in different costumes and poses.

◐ *Giambologna's* Rape of the Sabine Women, *in Piazza della Signoria*

Florence was an exciting place to be in the 15th century. The city's blossoming economy and its active writers, painters, architects and philosophers all made Florence a model of Renaissance culture. Leonardo da Vinci (1452–1519) was a prolific painter, architect and sculptor and also found time and talent to explore the world of invention and the study of anatomy and nature. Michelangelo stunned the world with his mammoth yet delicate statue *David*, now housed in the Accademia (see page 90).

The Carmelite friar Filippo Lippi reacted against this artistic strain, painting fantastical landscapes full of symbolism and flat, one-dimensional faces. Botticelli took up his ideas, creating allegorical, floating figures in an imaginary landscape.

Mannerism followed, with its highly stylised, brightly coloured, unnaturally shaped figures and scenes. Take a look at Andrea del Sarto's *Madonna of the Harpies* in the Uffizi, or the frescoes of Vasari (1511–74), which decorate the dome of the Duomo.

With so much art to admire, it would still be a pity to miss out on the other cultural attractions Florence has to offer. The city has several theatres which run full programmes of theatre, chamber music, opera and classical and modern dance. Modern artists are thriving and their works can be seen in private galleries around the city. To see what's on offer in the contemporary art scene, try checking out **Biagiotti Progetto Arte** (ⓐ Via delle Belle Donne 39r ⓣ 055 214 757 ⓦ www.artbiagiotti.com ⓛ 14.00–19.00 Tues–Sat).

○ *Ponte Vecchio, one of the city's most emblematic sights*

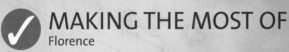

MAKING THE MOST OF
Florence

Shopping

Almost as big a draw as the museums and churches are Florence's shops, from the small, family-run businesses and craft workshops to the markets and larger stores. All the big-name Italian designers – Versace, Gucci, Armani, Ferragamo, Prada – as well as French designers have branches here and there are some good local department stores. The best shopping lies in a compact area of the inner city, so unless you want to make a real effort to visit the designer outlets in the city's industrial areas (see pages 12–13) you don't have to go far to find a good buy.

Most designer shops can be found in Via de' Tornabuoni and Via della Vigna Nuova. Oltrarno has lots of workshops where traditional crafts are still carried out, while Via Maggio and Via dei Fossi focus on antiques. Ponte Vecchio (see page 76) is the stairway to jewellery heaven, while San Lorenzo Market (see page 95) has good souvenirs and cheap clothes.

Shoe lovers will be at home in Florence. As well as the big names there are also tiny shops making beautiful footwear from Tuscan leather. Leather bags, belts, gloves and clothing are also handcrafted in the city and the best place to look is around the streets adjoining Piazza Santa Croce or the San Lorenzo market.

There are a few things that visitors might find unusual while shopping in Florence, especially in the smaller shops. Traditionally, if you go into a shop you are expected to announce what you are looking for and be shown examples of it. The sign *entrata libera/ingresso libero* means that you are welcome to browse with no compulsion to buy. You should also note Florentine opening hours (see page 145), which generally allow for a long lunch break in the early afternoon. Lots of small shops and the markets close completely for a period during the holiday months of July and August.

USEFUL SHOPPING PHRASES

What time do the shops open/close?
A che ora aprono/chiudono i negozi?
Ah keh ohrah ahprohnoh/kewdohnoh ee nehgotsee?

How much is this?
Quanto costa questo?
Kwantoh kostah kwestoh?

Can I try this on?   **My size is ...**
Posso provarlo?   La mia taglia è ...
Pohsoh prohvarloh?   *Lah meeyah tahlyah eh ...*

I'll take this one, thank you
Prenderò questo, grazie
Prehndehroh kwestoh, grahtsyeh

Can you show me the one in the window/this one?
Può mostrarmi quello in vetrina/questo?
Poh mohstrahrmee kwehloh een vehtreenah/kwestoh?

This is too large/too small/too expensive
Questo è troppo grande/troppo piccolo/troppo caro
Kwestoh eh trohpoh grahndeh/trohpoh peekohloh/trohpoh kahroh

Eating & drinking

Restaurants in Florence go by many names. A *trattoria* is generally more casual than an *osteria* or *ristorante*, although none of them have strict dress codes. A *pizzeria* is not so much a place that serves pizzas as a slightly cheaper and more casual *ristorante* with a similar menu. A *rosticceria* offers grilled meat along with the other standard dishes, often to take away as well as eat inside. *Tavola calda* indicates that the place is open at lunchtime for both hot and cold dishes. Besides these variations there are café-bars which offer a range of foods, from ready-cooked pastas to filled rolls, toasted breads and cakes.

In cheaper places with a bar, the food will generally cost less if you eat it standing at the bar than if you take a table. You may notice scales on the counter. Food such as pastas, pizza or focaccia will be sold to you by weight. Occasionally you tell the cashier what you want, pay for it, then take the bill to the counter to collect your food. Smoking is not allowed in restaurants (or any public places) unless there is a dedicated smoking room.

You may receive a stare of incomprehension if you ask about vegetarian options but don't worry – much of Italian cuisine is vegetarian without being identified as such. Check the pasta courses, which often feature seasonal vegetables and cheese, as well as the salads and vegetable dishes (*contorni*). Some excellent pizza options are purely vegetarian and there are Middle Eastern fast-food places

PRICE CATEGORIES
Based on a three-course meal for one person, without drinks.
£ up to €30   ££ €30–50   £££ over €50

WHAT'S ON THE MENU?

A full, traditional Tuscan meal is a relaxed, drawn-out affair with numerous courses. The meal starts with an *antipasto* (appetiser) such as cured meat, salami or pâté made from *cinghiale* (boar) or chicken liver. The meat usually comes served with *crostini*, tiny pieces of toasted or fried bread.

The *primo piatto* (starter) usually consists of pasta, risotto or soup. Sauces are often made with game, such as rabbit, hare, boar or pigeon. *Ravioli pecorino e pere* (ravioli stuffed with pear and pecorino cheese) is a Florentine speciality. Other dishes to try on this course are *panzanella*, made with day-old white bread, tomatoes, cucumber, red onion, basil and olive oil, and bruschetta, a Tuscan speciality based on grilled bread rubbed with garlic and served either plain or with a topping of tomatoes, garlic, basil and olive oil.

The *secondo piatto* (main course) is predominantly meat based, especially in winter. Warming stews of spiced rabbit or boar are typical, while *bistecca fiorentina*, T-bone steak cooked extremely rare, is served for two or three people. This dish comes with a *contorno* (side dish), which might be artichoke, French fries, white beans tossed in oil, boiled potatoes served with oil and pepper, or any one of a variety of salads involving wild rocket, radicchio, or even raw artichokes.

After the main course you can choose between various types of *formaggio* (cheese) – try pecorino, the Tuscan cheese made from sheep's milk – or a *dolce* (sweet dessert) such as a creamy tiramisu or a *panforte*, a thick jaw-gluing fruit cake. For a lighter option, ask for fresh fruit (*frutta*).

offering falafel. There are also some dedicated vegetarian restaurants. Try **Il Vegetariano** (🏠 Via delle Ruote 30r 📞 055 475 030 🕐 12.30–14.30 & 19.30–22.30 Tues–Fri, 19.30–22.30 Sat & Sun) or, for tasty Middle Eastern dishes based around fish and vegetables, head for **Ruth's** (🏠 Via Farini 2a 📞 055 248 0888 🌐 www.kosheruth.com 🕐 12.30–15.00 & 19.00–22.30 Mon–Thur, 12.30–15.00 Fri; also 19.00–22.30 Sat, Oct–Apr).

USEFUL DINING PHRASES

I would like a table for ... people
Vorrei un tavolo per ... persone
Vohray oon tahvohloh pehr ... pehrsohneh

May I have the bill, please?
Mi dà il conto, per favore?
Mee dah eel cohntoh, pehr fahvohreh?

Excuse me!
Scusi!
Skoozee!

Could I have it well cooked/medium/rare, please?
Potrei averlo ben cotto/mediamente cotto/al sangue, per favore?
Pohtray ahvehrloh behn kohtoh/mehdyahmehnteh kohtoh/ ahl sahngweh, pehr fahvohreh?

I am a vegetarian. Does this contain meat?
Sono vegetariano/vegetariana. Contiene carne?
Sohnoh vehjehtehrehahnoh/vehjehtehrehahnah. Kontyehneh kahrneh?

Tuscany is a major producer of both red and white wine, the most famous of which is Chianti. In recent years, winegrowers have introduced French grapes to Tuscan vineyards and Tuscan wine has become so complex that *enoturismo* (wine tourism) is now an entire industry, with visitors touring the vineyards of Tuscany and tasting the wines. See Ⓦ www.movimentoturismovino.it

Common *aperitivos* (pre-dinner drinks) are Campari or Prosecco. To end a meal ask for a *digestívo* such as *grappa*, or a sweet liqueur such as *limoncello*.

Coffee drinking in Florence follows certain rules. Cappuccino is drunk only in the morning with breakfast and is usually served warm but not scalding. Espresso is drunk during the day and after dinner and may include a shot of spirits. Other coffee options are *caffè americano,* which is espresso diluted with water, or *caffè macchiato*, which is espresso with hot or cold milk added.

🔺 *Bruschetta is a simple but delicious Tuscan speciality*

Entertainment & nightlife

Florence, alongside its historical and cultural nature, has a loud and thriving nightlife. Live music is popular in the city, particularly jazz and Latin American music. The big live music shows are usually held in the **Palasport Mandela Forum** (ⓐ Viale Malta 6 ❶ 055 678 841) or in the smaller **Saschall-Teatro di Firenze** (ⓐ Lungarno Aldo Moro 3 ❶ 055 650 4112), both outside the centre. **Sala Vanni** (ⓐ Piazza del Carmine ⓦ www.musicusconcentus.com) often plays host to jazz and classical performances. Occasionally the football stadium (see page 32) accommodates the really big megastars.

Smaller places which have regular live music include the Astor Café (see page 97) and the **Latin American Girasol** (ⓐ Via del Romito 1, outside the city gates ❶ 055 474 948 ⓦ www.girasol.it ❷ 20.00–02.30 Tues–Sun). Jazz Club (see page 71) has live jazz

nightly. In summer there are open-air jazz sessions in **Piazza della Santissima Annunziata**.

Classical music also thrives in Florence. Opera was allegedly invented here and there are regular opera performances in the city at **Teatro del Maggio Musicale Fiorentino** (ⓐ Via Solferino 15 ☎ 055 277 9350 ⓦ www.maggiofiorentino.com), which also hosts performances of classical and modern ballet and theatrical productions. For opera you can also try **Teatro Goldoni** (ⓐ Via di Santa Maria 15 ☎ 055 210 804), while the **Lutheran Church** (ⓐ Lungarno Torrigiani 11) has regular, free concerts of organ and chamber music.

The theatre is generally aimed at Italian speakers, so it can be difficult for visitors. Most productions take place between September and April. For visiting theatre productions, see **Teatro della Pergola** (ⓐ Via della Pergola 12–13, San Marco ☎ 055 226 4353

● *The city shimmers and glows by night*

TICKETS & INFORMATION

To buy tickets for most productions in the city, visit **Box Office** ⓐ Via Alammani 39, Santa Maria Novella ⓣ 055 210 804 ⓦ www.boxol.it ⓛ 10.00–19.30 Mon–Sat

For information on what's on, check with the English-language paper *The Florentine* (ⓦ www.theflorentine.net) or with the *Firenze Spettacolo* (ⓦ www.firenzespettacolo.it).

ⓦ www.teatrodellapergola.com). Dance has a more international appeal and performances of ballet and modern dance take place regularly at the **Teatro del Maggio** (contact details page 29).

Films in Florence are for the most part dubbed into Italian. For English-language films go to **Odeon Original Sound** (ⓐ Via dei Sassetti 1 ⓣ 055 214 068 ⓦ www.cinehall.it), a beautiful Art Nouveau cinema. **Cinecittà** (ⓐ Via Baccio da Montelupo 35 ⓣ 055 732 4510) occasionally has English-language or subtitled films but you must have a membership card.

A good way to start an evening is with an *aperitivo* – a light, alcoholic drink often served with a substantial snack – in a trendy café-bar. For a noisy night, there are plenty of pubs aimed at young tourists and students, which offer special deals on drinks or even free drinks for ladies mid-week. There are also many upmarket places for more discerning customers.

The city's clubs in particular have metamorphosed in recent years. Like the café-bars they serve food during the day, changing at night into cleverly lit, stylish places offering cosy seating areas and chill-out rooms. In summer, clubs, bars and restaurants often find an outside space to operate in, especially along the river and in the squares or a park.

🔺 *Grab an early-evening* aperitivo *at Loggia del Pesce*

Sport & relaxation

Florence isn't the first place that comes to mind when planning a sports holiday, but there are plenty of sporting possibilities around the city, including the annual marathon.

SPECTATOR SPORTS
Football
Stadio Artemio Franchi is the home of Florence's football team, Fiorentina. Tickets can be bought online or at the stadium. ⓐ Campo di Marte, outside the city gates ⓣ 055 503 0190 ⓦ http://it.violachannel.tv ⓛ Aug–May, usually every other Sun ⓝ Bus: 3, 11, 17

Horse racing
Ippodromo delle Cascine is based in Cascine Park, outside the city gates, and regularly holds flat-race meetings. If you just want to see the horses, go early in the morning to watch them practising. ⓐ Via delle Cascine 3, Parco delle Cascine ⓣ 055 422 6076 ⓦ www.ippodromifiorentini.it ⓛ Apr–May & Sept–Oct ⓝ Bus: 17C

Motor racing
Autodromo del Mugello is a prominent feature in the world of motorsport and regular meetings are held here. On quiet days motorcyclists can bring their bike and try out the circuit. ⓣ 055 849 9111 ⓦ www.mugellocircuit.it ⓛ Mar–Nov

PARTICIPATION SPORTS
Juggling
JokoL'arte Juggling Store Pick up juggling balls, Diablo or choose from a huge range of unicycles. ⓐ Via degli Alfani 5lr ⓣ 055 244 789

Ⓦ www.jokolarte.com Ⓛ 10.30–13.00 & 16.00–19.30 Tues–Fri, 10.30–13.00 & 16.00–19.00 Sat

Roller-skating

Le Pavoniere in Cascine Park provides skate hire. ⓐ Viale della Catena 2, Parco delle Cascine Ⓣ 335 571 8547 Ⓛ 15.00–20.00 Tues–Thur, 10.00–20.00 Sat & Sun Ⓝ Bus: 17C

Squash

Centro Squash Firenze Squash courts, gym, sauna and equipment hire. ⓐ Via Empoli 16 Ⓣ 055 732 3055 Ⓦ www.centrosquashfirenze. com Ⓛ 09.30–23.00 Mon–Fri, 10.30–18.00 Sat Ⓝ Bus: 1

Swimming

Piscina Bellariva Olympic-size pool in a park to the east of the city. Smaller pool for children. ⓐ Lungarno Aldo Moro 6, outside the city gates Ⓣ 055 677 521 Ⓛ 10.00–18.00 daily (mid-June–mid-Sept); 10.00–18.00 & 20.30–23.00 Tues & Thur, 10.00–18.00 Wed & Fri–Mon (mid-Sept–mid-June)

Trekking & walking

Gruppo Escursionistico Club Alpino Italiano organises treks through the Tuscan hills on Sundays. ⓐ Via del Mezzetta 2, outside the city gates Ⓣ 055 612 0467 Ⓦ www.caifirenze.it

Walking Tours of Florence offers a range of walking tours of the city, arranging entry to museums and meals. Bicycle tours of Tuscany also available. ⓐ Via dei Sassetti 1 Ⓣ 055 264 5033 Ⓦ www.italy.artviva.com Ⓛ 08.00–18.00 Mon–Sat, mornings only Sun

Accommodation

There are various official categories of accommodation in Florence. To be classed as a hotel and get an official one- to five-star rating, an establishment must have seven or more rooms. Smaller places are *affitacamere* (rooms for rent), which can be anything from a bed and breakfast to just that – a room in someone's house. *Residenza d'epoca* is a B&B in a listed building. Confusingly, the term 'residence' refers chiefly to self-catering apartments.

There are many hotels in the city, with many of the larger two- and three-star places catering for tour groups. Be aware that tour groups tend to get up and go down to breakfast at the same time, so hot water and tables may be scarce if you coincide with them.

A continental breakfast is usually included in the room rate, but do check in advance.

The peak tourist season runs from late March to July. Hotels tend to be full and also charge more, so book early and look out for special deals. In the very hot months of late July and August prices fall sharply, then rise again when the weather cools in September. If you visit in low season, you may be able to get a sizeable discount on accommodation. Useful contacts are:

Consorzio Florence Promhotels for hotel bookings ☎ 055 553 941 ⓦ www.promhotels.it

PRICE CATEGORIES
Ratings are based on the average price per night of a room for two people with breakfast.
£ up to €75   ££ €75–150   £££ over €150

⬥ *Immerse yourself in local life by renting an apartment*

Associazione Bed & Breakfast e Affittacamere for B&Bs
 199 445 982  www.anbba.it

HOTELS

Hotel Orchidea £ Simple rooms, mostly with hand basins in the
rooms rather than en-suite. Very inexpensive.  Borgo degli Albizi 11
 055 248 0346  www.hotelorchideaflorence.it  Bus: 14, 23

Casci £–££ Friendly small hotel in a 15th-century *palazzo* with lots of
reading material, an open-plan bar and breakfast room, plus simple
but well-maintained bedrooms.  Via Cavour 13  055 211 686
 055 239 6461  www.hotelcasci.com  Bus: C1, 14, 23

Annalena ££ Small three-star hotel in a quiet area south of Palazzo
Pitti. Antiques, a garden and thoughtful staff make this a good
alternative to city-centre hotels.  Via Romana 34  055 222 402
 055 222 403  www.hotelannalena.it  Bus: 36, 37

Bellettini ££ Two-star hotel with 27 rooms, some with TVs and
private bathrooms. All rooms have air conditioning. Great breakfast.
 Via dei Conti 7  055 213 561  055 283 551  www.hotel
bellettini.com  Bus: C2

Morandi alla Crocetta ££ Small, friendly three-star hotel run by
English-speaking staff. Pleasant rooms, some with original medieval
frescoes, antiques and views over the garden.  Via Laura 50  055 234
4747  055 248 0954  www.hotelmorandi.it  Bus: C1, 6, 32

Gallery Hotel Art £££ Florence's first designer hotel is located just
west of Ponte Vecchio. Book one of the three penthouses for a

weekend of extravagance. ⓐ Vicolo dell'Oro 5 ① 055 27263
① 055 268 557 ⓦ www.lungarnohotels.com Ⓝ Bus: C3

Grand Hotel Minerva £££ Conveniently located in Piazza Santa
Maria Novella, this modern, bright hotel has comfortable rooms,
views over the square or over the church and a small pool and bar
on the roof. In summer the restaurant moves out on to the square.
ⓐ Piazza Santa Maria Novella 16 ① 055 27230 ① 055 268 281
ⓦ www.grandhotelminerva.com Ⓝ Bus: 36, 37

Grand Hotel Villa Medici £££ The hotel is in an 18th-century villa
with private grounds, decorated inside with antiques. Rooms have
all the modern conveniences imaginable and some have whirlpool
baths and balconies. The hotel has a pool and is just outside the
city walls, behind Santa Maria Novella. Excellent buffet breakfast.
ⓐ Via Il Prato 42 ① 055 277 171 ① 055 238 1336 ⓦ www.villamedici
hotel.com Ⓝ Bus: C2, D

Villa La Vedetta £££ Extreme luxury on the top of Viale Michelangelo.
This hotel, converted from two private villas, is set in its own gardens,
with two pools and the most amazing views in the city. There is
a fitness room and sauna and the guest rooms are well equipped
with Wi-Fi and an Internet connection via the flat-screen TV.
ⓐ Viale Michelangelo 78 ① 055 681 631 ① 055 658 2544
ⓦ www.villalavedettahotel.com Ⓝ Bus: 12, 13

APARTMENTS & B&BS
Residenza Johanna Uno £ Excellent value in this well-run, small
and cosy B&B, close to Museo San Marco. ⓐ Via Bonifacio Lupi 14
① 055 481 896 ① 055 482 721 ⓦ www.johanna.it Ⓝ Bus: 8

◆ *For luxury, you can't beat Villa La Vedetta*

One World Apartments £–££ Book one of these attractive renovated apartments for a taste of true Florentine life. Dotted around the city centre, they often offer last-minute discounts. ❸ Check-in: Via della Vigna Nuova 9 ❶ 055 274 871 ❿ www.one-real-world.com ❷ Bus: 6, 11, 22, 36, 37, 68

Residenza d'Epoca in Piazza della Signoria £££ Graceful B&B with ten individually designed rooms, many overlooking the square, and three apartments. Breakfast is a shared table or can be eaten privately in your room. Internet, hot water for drinks and lots of friendly advice and assistance. ❸ Via dei Magazzini 2 ❶ 055 239 9546 ❺ 055 267 6616 ❿ www.inpiazzadellasignoria.com ❷ Bus: C1, C2

HOSTELS & CAMPSITES

Camping Michelangelo £ Close to Piazzale Michelangelo and with amazing views. Bring your own tent or hire a 'house tent' with beds. There is a bar, restaurant, supermarket and disco. It can get crowded in the summer, so visit away from the peak season if possible. ❸ Viale Michelangelo 80 ❶ 055 681 1977 ❺ 055 689 348 ❿ www.ecvacanze.it ❷ Bus: 12, 13

Ostello Villa Camerata £ Formerly a 17th-century private home. Set in a massive green park, encircled by botanic gardens, the Ostello Villa Camerata is an oasis of calm. ❸ Viale Righi 2/4 ❶ 055 601 451 ❺ 055 610 300 ❿ www.ostellofirenze.it ❷ Bus: 17

THE BEST OF FLORENCE

Whether you are on a flying visit to Florence or taking a more leisurely break in northern Italy, the city and its surroundings offer some sights, places and experiences that should not be missed. For the best attractions for children, see pages 145–7.

TOP 10 ATTRACTIONS

- **The Uffizi** Home to some of the most moving and beautiful works of art in the world (see pages 64–5).

- **The Duomo** Because size matters (see pages 85–6).

- **Santa Maria Novella** Admire the beautiful Renaissance frescoes (see pages 76–7).

- **Museo San Marco** Where Savonarola lived and where Fra Angelico's beautiful paintings still retain their original simplicity and intensity (see page 92).

- **Ponte Vecchio** Where all that glitters probably is gold (see page 76).

- **Walking or cycling tour of the city** Get the feel of the medieval streets beneath your feet in the company of a guide who knows the city well (see page 33).

- **Mercato Centrale** Where you can buy anything from a whole pecorino cheese to a new leather outfit (see page 95).

- **Michelangelo's *David*** An inspiring, passionate creature carved from a vast piece of marble (see page 90).

- **Piazzale Michelangelo** Get out of town, enjoy the fresh air and admire the views of the whole city (see page 100).

- **A night on the town** Start off with aperitifs in Dolce Vita (see page 110) and work your way back to town, ending up at the Jazz Club (see page 71) for some soothing live jazz.

● *Florence's ancient city skyline*

Suggested itineraries

HALF-DAY: FLORENCE IN A HURRY

Book in advance to get priority entrance to the Uffizi (see pages 64–5). Head straight for the *Primavera* and the *Birth of Venus*, probably the best of Botticelli's many works, then have a look at Titian's *Urbino Venus*. Head out to Mercato Nuovo (see page 72), rub the snout of the bronze boar in the Il Porcellino fountain in order to return to the city, then swing south to Ponte Vecchio (see page 76). Get a taxi up to Piazzale Michelangelo (see page 100) and take your camera.

1 DAY: TIME TO SEE A LITTLE MORE

Spend longer in the Uffizi and really appreciate the great art it contains. Pre-book the Accademia (see page 90) and marvel at *David* before taking in Michelangelo's other works. Lunch at Rivoire in Piazza della Signoria (see page 68) or one of the cafés in Piazza della Repubblica. Check out the market and Ponte Vecchio and head on to Palazzo Pitti (see pages 102–3) to wonder at the brash Medici riches. As dusk approaches, walk across Ponte alle Grazie and take a photo of Ponte Vecchio with the setting sun behind it. Walk quickly up to Piazzale Michelangelo to take in the gorgeous nightscapes and treat yourself with a meal at one of the city's many atmospheric restaurants.

2–3 DAYS: TIME TO SEE MUCH MORE

Add the Bargello (see page 65) to your list of museums and check out Museo San Marco (see page 92), San Lorenzo (see pages 88–9) and Santa Croce (see pages 62–4). The Museo Galileo (see page 147) makes a pleasant change from all the art and you can explore some of the small streets around Santa Croce and the Mercato Centrale (see page 95), checking out the leather workshops and restaurants.

The streets between the Duomo, the river and the railway station are filled with gorgeous little shops.

LONGER: ENJOYING FLORENCE TO THE FULL

There is time to get out for a proper exploration of Oltrarno (see pages 98–110), the Bóboli Gardens (see pages 98–101), the weird and wonderful wax museum La Specola (see page 102) and to enjoy dinner in one of the squares on the south side of the river. Consider a day trip to Siena (see pages 126–38) for its medieval feel and quieter atmosphere. Visit Pisa (see pages 112–25) and pose for a classic photo pretending to hold up the tower. If you're not overdosed on art, seek out some of Florence's smaller churches, such as Ognissanti (see pages 72–5) or Orsanmichele (see page 44).

⬤ *Bóboli Gardens has plenty of attractive water features*

Something for nothing

Life can be expensive in Florence. Most museums have an entrance charge and some charge an additional fee to jump the queue. Even churches may charge quite high prices to pay for upkeep. But Florence does offer a fair range of activities at no cost whatsoever.

For those with strong willpower, window-shopping is one inexpensive way to spend an afternoon. The views from Piazzale Michelangelo (see page 100) are completely free, as is the walk through pleasant parkland up to it. Visit Parco delle Cascine to check out the football matches and enjoy a bit of people-watching. Take a stroll along the river. The city's markets are a worthwhile experience and touching the snout of the bronze boar in Mercato Nuovo (see page 72) costs nothing but will, they say, one day bring you back to the city.

Many important artworks are in the city streets and can be viewed at no expense. Look up at street corners to see frescoes installed by the city's ancient guilds, or wander through Piazza della Signoria to see an amazing collection of statues.

The following do not charge an entrance fee:

Biblioteca Medicea-Laurenziana This was built to hold the Medici manuscripts and has a staircase designed by Michelangelo (see page 89).

Ognissanti Amazing atmosphere and a Botticelli (see pages 72–5).

Orsanmichele Beautiful exterior and elaborate tabernacle inside. Next door is the **Museo di Orsanmichele**, also free and full of statues removed from the exterior. ❸ Via dell'Arte della Lana ❶ 055 210 305 ❶ 10.00–17.00 daily

San Miniato al Monte A lovely church with spectacular views over the city (see page 103).

Santa Felicità (see pages 105–6).

Santa Trinità A 13th-century church, the highlight of which is the Cappella Sassetti covered in frescoes by Ghirlandaio. One of these is set in the Piazza della Signoria and includes portraits of Lorenzo the Magnificent and his children (see page 75).

Santissima Annunziata Church with a painting allegedly finished by an angel while the artist slept (see page 89).

Santo Spirito A fine church and Brunelleschi's last work (see page 103).

🔺 *The green and white inlaid marble façade of San Miniato al Monte*

When it rains

The city's narrow streets can occasionally make a rainy day seem like a battleground. There is rarely room for two umbrella-wielding pedestrians to pass and dodging a poke in the eye can be quite tricky. It's lucky that so much of what people come to see in the city is indoors.

A good place to queue in the rain is at the Uffizi (see pages 64–5), where the queue stands under a loggia and people are entertained for hours by buskers and pavement artists. The Uffizi has the added bonus of an amazing series of shops selling innovative versions of its works of art – Primavera jigsaws, Rembrandt coffee mugs, Urbino Venus plastic aprons as well as some excellent books, beautiful shawls and even some jewellery modelled on designs from some of the more famous paintings. The Uffizi has another advantage – you are inside for so long (making sure the queuing was worth it) that by the time you come out it's time to slink off to a café and watch the rain from inside.

The Bargello (see page 65) is another good place to visit in the rain. The queues are much shorter here and the lobby holds most of the people who want to buy a ticket. Its inner courtyard is open to the sky but the route between the rooms is covered. Really appreciating the collection of statues in each of the rooms takes a long time – perfect if the alternative is getting wet.

A trip to the cinema that shows English-language films (see page 30) is a good way to spend a rainy evening. Sitting under the protective canopy at Rivoire (see page 68) or one of the city's other atmospheric cafés, drinking hot chocolate and watching other people getting wet, is a pleasant experience at any time of day.

◭ *The soaring tower of the Uffizi*

On arrival

TIME DIFFERENCE

Italy follows Central European Time (CET), which is one hour
ahead of Greenwich Mean Time (GMT). Clocks go forward
one hour at the end of March and fall back one hour at the
end of October.

ARRIVING
By air

Most travellers will arrive either at Florence's own airport, or at
Pisa International Airport and transfer into Florence.

IF YOU GET LOST, TRY ...

Excuse me, do you speak English?
Mi scusi, parla inglese?
Mee scoozee, pahrlah eenglehzeh?

**Excuse me, is this the right way to the old town/the city
centre/the tourist office/the station/the bus station?**
Mi scusi, questa è la strada giusta per la città vecchia/il centro/
l'ufficio informazioni turistiche/la stazione ferroviaria/
la stazione degli autobus?
*Mee skoozee, kwestah eh lah strahdah justah pehr lah cheetah
vehkyah/eel chentroh/loofeecho eenfohrmahtsyonee
tooreesteekeh/lah stahtsyoneh fehrohveeahreeyah/lah
stahtsyoneh dehlyee owtohboos?*

Florence's airport is **Aeroporto di Firenze** (ⓐ Amerigo Vespucci ⓣ 055 306 1300 ⓦ www.aeroporto.firenze.it). It is about 5 km (3 miles) west of the city centre, linked to the city by buses which run every half-hour from 06.00–23.30 and arrive at the **SITA bus station** at Via Santa Caterina da Siena (ⓣ 800 424 500 ⓦ www.sitabus.it). Taxis are more expensive (around €20) and take about 15 minutes.

Pisa Galileo Galilei Airport (ⓣ 050 849 111 ⓦ www.pisa-airport.com) is connected by direct rail link to Santa Maria Novella station in Florence. Trains run between 06.40 and 22.20 and take about 1 hour and 20 minutes. There are also three trains an hour from the airport to Pisa's central station.

A third possibility is to travel on the **Terravision bus** (ⓦ www.lowcostcoach.com) from Pisa airport to Florence's Santa Maria Novella train station. Tickets are available in the main concourse and journey time is about the same as the train. The bus timetable is geared to the arrival times of low-cost flights. If a flight is delayed, the bus will usually wait.

By train

Florence's main railway station is **Santa Maria Novella** (ⓛ 04.15–01.30 daily, information office 07.00–21.00 daily, ticket office 05.50–22.00 daily). The city centre is within walking distance if you are not carrying heavy bags, or you can take a taxi.

There are two other major stations in the city, both connected to Santa Maria Novella with a journey time of five minutes. **Campo di Marte** serves the northeast and **Firenze Rifredi** serves the northwest.

General information ⓣ 892 021 (from within Italy only) ⓦ www.ferroviedellostato.it

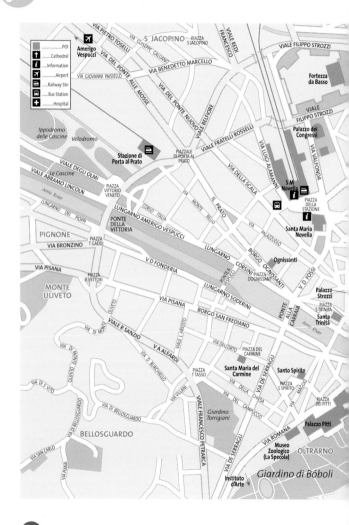

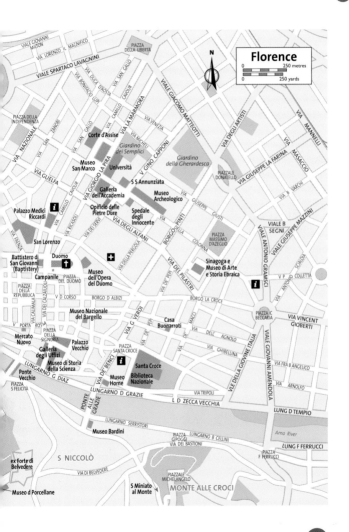

By road

SITA buses from around Tuscany (🅦 www.sitabus.it) arrive at their terminal just outside Santa Maria Novella station.

Traffic in the city centre is strictly limited during the day to public transport and permit holders, although hire cars are allowed to drive to hotels. In summer traffic is banned in some areas altogether, indicated by digital signs along inbound roads. If you have a car, choose a hotel outside the restricted zone and be prepared to pay high parking fees. Check 🅦 www.firenzeparcheggi.it for information about parking.

FINDING YOUR FEET

As in other busy cities, take the obvious precautions to avoid pickpocketing and petty fraud, particularly in touristy areas, and lock up all your valuables in your hotel. Avoid the area around the railway station late at night; in general other areas are perfectly safe.

At pedestrian crossings, look carefully to make sure there is no traffic coming (including from side roads), then be bold and step clearly into the street. If you hesitate, cars will simply swerve past you. You should be careful even when the green 'walk' or *avanti* signal is showing as drivers turning into the road may ignore it.

ORIENTATION

Taking the Duomo as the focal point, Via dei Calzaiuoli runs south towards Piazza della Signoria and the river. Via de' Cerretani leads west towards the railway station. East of the Duomo, roads bend south towards Piazza Santa Croce. North of the Duomo lie San Marco and San Lorenzo. South of the river is Oltrarno and the Palazzo Pitti.

It's a good idea to acquire a detailed map, preferably with a street index, from a newsstand, bookshop or the tourist office.

GETTING AROUND

Florence is such a small city that for most people there is hardly any
need for public transport. Although public transport references have
been given in this guidebook wherever possible, it is usually much
easier to walk to your destination.

The ATAF (Ⓦ www.ataf.net) bus lines are useful if you do need
a ride in the centre. There are four electric bus services, the Bussini
Ecologici, which make small circuits of the city:

⬥ The Neptune Fountain, Piazza della Signoria

Bus C1 travels from Piazza della Repubblica, through Via Roma, Via de' Tavolini, east along Via Ghibellina, up Via Verdi and west along Via Bufalini north of the Duomo. It then turns north up Via Cavour and travels up to Piazza della Libertà before returning south along Via La Marmora. It makes a loop travelling back west along Via dell'Oriuolo to the Duomo, turns down Via Proconsolo and goes along Via Condotta before returning to Piazza della Repubblica.

Bus C2 starts at the Stazione Leopolda near Porta al Prato, goes to the station, then to the Duomo where it turns south, passes by Piazza della Repubblica, along Via de' Tavolini and east towards Piazza Beccaria. It then heads back into the centre of town via Via dell'Agnolo and Via dell'Oriuolo. It returns to its starting point via the station, Via Palazzuolo and Via Solferino.

Bus C3 also starts at the Stazione Leopolda and travels east, crossing the river at Ponte alla Carraia. It continues east along Borgo San Jacopo and Via de' Bardi, where it recrosses the Arno and goes past Santa Croce to Piazza Beccaria. It passes Santa Croce again on its way back south of the river and then passes Ponte Vecchio, Palazzo Pitti and Via Maggio before turning west, back to the start point.

Bus D mainly serves the Oltrarno but starts on the south side of Piazza della Stazione. It crosses Ponte Vespucci and travels along Borgo San Frediano, Lungarno Guicciardini, Borgo San Jacopo and Via de' Bardi before arriving at Piazza Ferrucci to the east. It then heads back to the station via Lungarno Serristori, Ponte Vecchio, Piazza dei Pitti, Piazza Santo Spirito and Piazza del Carmine.

Regular ATAF buses 12 and 13 make a circuit of the city (in opposite directions) and are useful for getting to Oltrarno and Piazzale Michelangelo. Bus 7 travels from Santa Maria Novella to Piazza San Marco and then north out of town. Bus 70 is a night bus serving Santa Maria Novella station, the city centre and Campo di Marte.

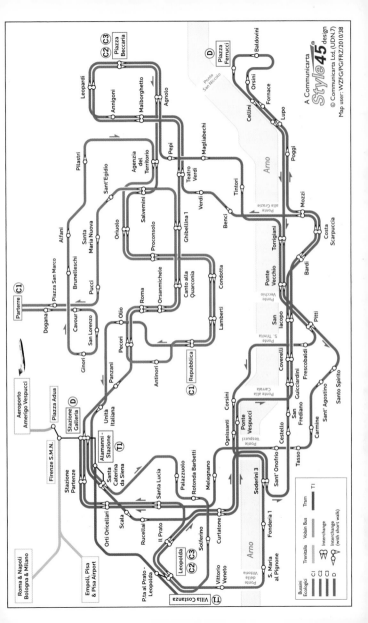

Buses run from about 05.30–21.00 every 10–30 minutes but don't stick to a strict timetable. Tickets can be bought from newsstands, bars or tobacconists displaying the bus company sign ATAF. You must validate your ticket in the machine at the front of the bus. Tickets last three hours, so they can be used to change buses or for a second or third journey if it is within the time limit.

Taxis cannot be flagged down in the street. You must find a taxi rank or phone for one. When you phone, you will be given a code name and a number which will be on the door of the taxi – beware, as the meter starts running as soon as the taxi starts its journey towards you. The minimum fare is around €5 to €9, depending on the time of day. There are extra charges if you've called a cab rather than picking it up at a rank, if you have luggage that must be stored in the boot, or if it's a public holiday.

There are taxi ranks in Piazza della Repubblica, Piazza della Stazione, Piazza Santa Maria Novella, Piazza del Duomo, Piazza San Marco, Piazza Santa Croce and Piazza Santa Trinità. To book a taxi, call:
Radio Taxi ❶ 055 4390, 055 4798
So.Co.Ta. ❶ 055 4242 Ⓦ www.socota.it

Car hire

Although hiring a car for travel within the city would not be recommended, you may choose to rent a car to explore Tuscany. The best spot to pick up hire cars is at the airport. Book in advance – car shortages and very high same-day fees are relatively common.
Avis ❶ 055 289 010, 055 213 629 Ⓦ www.avis.com
Hertz ❶ 055 239 8205, 055 282 260 Ⓦ www.hertz.com
Maggiore ❶ 055 311 256 Ⓦ www.maggiore.it

◗ *The striking sight of the Duomo above the Florentine skyline*

THE CITY OF
Florence

The Uffizi & east

This is the tourist heart of Florence, with Piazza della Signoria at its centre, and visitors here often outnumber locals. Street artists and musicians will compete with the museums to relieve you of your cash but don't let this put you off. There's a reason so many people flock here and as you wander through the Uffizi or the Bargello Museum, encountering so many icons of Western culture, the majesty of the place becomes clear.

Restaurants abound, with lots of them in the little streets snaking eastwards past Santa Croce. If you prefer to eat alfresco, seek out the huge supermarket **Standa** (ⓐ Via Pietrapiana), with its excellent bakery and picnic essentials.

Like most of Florence's city centre, it is easy and practical to access the area on foot and many areas are entirely pedestrianised. Should you need public transport to access the area, hop on Bus A. Bus B runs along the south side of this area and Bus C along the eastern edge.

SIGHTS & ATTRACTIONS

Museo di Storia della Scienza (Museum of the History of Science)

The 16th-century physicist, inventor and astronomer Galileo spent time in Florence under the patronage of the Medici family after he was excommunicated by the Catholic Church. The museum contains much of his equipment, including the lens he used to identify the moon of Jupiter. It also, for some reason, contains one of his finger bones, plus lots of beautifully made instruments. There are occasional demonstrations of his experiments.

ⓐ Piazza dei Giudici ⓣ 055 265 311 ⓦ www.museogalileo.it

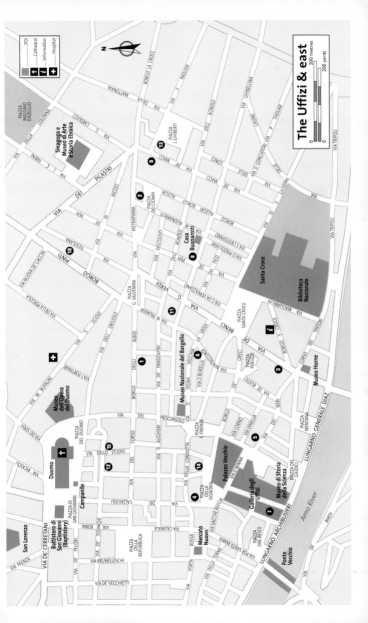

⬤ *A copy of* David *stands outside the Palazzo Vecchio*

🕐 09.30–13.00 Tues, 09.30–18.00 Wed–Mon Ⓝ Bus: C3, 23
ⓘ Admission charge

Palazzo Vecchio (Old Palace)

The Palazzo Vecchio, the seat of the city's government, was designed by Arnolfo di Cambio and built between 1298 and 1314. The original medieval interior was renovated by the Medici family in the 16th century and its appearance today is largely according to their taste.

The Salone dei Cinquecento (Hall of the Five Hundred) on the first floor was named after the Council, which had five hundred members. It was intended to be covered in frescoes by Leonardo da Vinci and Michelangelo, but Leonardo didn't get round to it and Michelangelo got a better offer from the Pope. The work was done by Vasari instead, although Michelangelo's *Victory* statue is displayed here.

Next door, peek into the Studiolo di Francesco I, decorated with frescoes of an alchemist's laboratory and the sciences. On the second floor in the Quartiere degli Elementi (Room of the Elements), Vasari has depicted the four elements air, earth, fire and water, while the six rooms of the Quartiere de Eleonora – the apartments of Cosimo I's wife – are decorated with scenes of virtuous women. The Sala dei Gigli (Room of the Lilies) contains, among other things, Donatello's *Judith and Holofernes*. The bell tower beside the *palazzo* is the city's highest at 94 m (308 ft) and houses the prison room where Savonarola (see page 62) spent the last days of his life.

Guided tours of the *palazzo* take you into rooms and passageways not accessible to the general public, last an hour and a half, and are well worth the extra cost. English tours are popular so be sure to book in advance. ⓐ Piazza della Signoria ☎ 055 276 8465
🕐 09.00–14.00 Thur, 09.00–19.00 Fri–Wed Ⓝ Bus: C1, C2
ⓘ Admission charge

Santa Croce

A survivor of medieval times, this originally simple church was built in 1228 by the newly established order of Franciscans. They were

STATUES IN THE PIAZZA

Originally a forecourt to the Palazzo Vecchio in 1307, the Piazza della Signoria became the place where Florence's ruling families put on a show of wealth in the form of statues of themselves and other great works by sculptors. Most of these have now been brought inside out of the weather and replaced by replicas, but they are still worth admiring.

Take a look at the replica of Michelangelo's *David* (the original is in the Galleria dell'Accademia, see page 90), the equestrian statue of Cosimo I and a rather overwrought fountain featuring Neptune by Ammannati. Nearby you'll see Donatello's heraldic lion *Marzocco* and his *Judith and Holofernes. Hercules and Cacus* by Bandinelli sit on the steps opposite the *Marzocco*. You can also see Cellini's bronze statue of *Perseus* holding the Medusa's head as well as the *Rape of the Sabine Women*, a tortuously writhing piece carved out of a single block of marble by Giambologna in 1583.

As you wander the square admiring these works of art you might think back to the day in 1497 when the anti-Renaissance priest Savonarola lit his Bonfire of the Vanities here. He destroyed what would now be a priceless collection of art, yet was aided and abetted by some of the artists themselves. A year later Savonarola stood tied to a stake in the exact same spot, burning as a heretic.

founded as an order that espoused poverty, but by the end of the century they were as rich and worldly as any other religious order and wanted to show off their wealth by building a flash new church. It was designed by Arnolfo di Cambio, who also designed the Duomo and the Palazzo Vecchio.

The church is home to the tombs of a host of medieval and Renaissance figures, including Michelangelo, Galileo, Ghiberti and Machiavelli. The frescoes in the Bardi and Peruzzi chapels are by

◆ *Keep your eyes peeled for sun-dappled courtyards hidden away inside* palazzi

Giotto and depict the lives of St John the Baptist, St Francis and St John the Evangelist. In the Baroncelli chapel, the fresco by Gaddi is thought to be the first night scene ever depicted in a fresco.

Within the church is the entrance to Cappella dei Pazzi, a little domed chapel designed by Brunelleschi. This in turn leads into the cloisters, a haven from all the marble and artworks of the church. Across the courtyard is a little museum of church art, including some modern pieces by Pietro Parigi. ⓐ Piazza Santa Croce ⓘ 055 246 6105 ⓛ 09.30–17.30 Mon–Sat, 13.00–17.30 Sun ⓦ Bus: 23, C3 ⓘ Admission charge

CULTURE

Casa Buonarroti (Buonarroti House)

The house where Michelangelo never lived. His descendants did live here though, and they collected memorabilia and a couple of good pieces – a bas-relief *Madonna* and an unfinished *Battle of the Centaurs*, both the work of the artist during his adolescence. ⓐ Via Ghibellina 70 ⓘ 055 241 752 ⓦ www.casabuonarroti.it ⓛ 09.30–16.00 Wed–Mon ⓦ Bus: C2, C3 ⓘ Admission charge

Galleria degli Uffizi (Uffizi Gallery)

Housed in a 16th-century palace built by Vasari for Cosimo I, the Uffizi boasts one of the finest art collections in the world. It was actually the personal art collection of several generations of the Medici family, starting with Francesco I in the 16th century. The last of their line, Anna Maria Lodovica, bequeathed it to the state.

Filippo Lippi and his pupil Botticelli are well represented, as are Michelangelo, Raphael, Titian, Leonardo, Mantegna, Caravaggio, Tiepolo, Rembrandt, Goya – it might be easier to list which of the world's greatest artists aren't represented here. Just steaming past the most famous artworks will take you about two hours.

The Uffizi is vast and hugely popular. To make the most of your visit, book ahead to avoid the long queue, bring a floor plan with you and make sure you know what you want to see. Or you can book a tour with one of many companies that will guide you through the highlights.

For a break go out on to the Loggia de Lanzi terrace, where you are right under the *campanile* (bell tower) of the Palazzo Vecchio and can admire the clock face close up. ❸ Piazzale degli Uffizi 4–6 ❶ 055 238 8651 (info), 055 294 883 (reservations) ❿ www.uffizi.firenze.it ❶ 08.15–22.00 Tues, 08.15–18.50 Wed–Sun (July–Sept); 08.15–18.50 Tues–Sun (Oct–June) ❿ Bus: C1, C2, D, 23 ❶ Admission charge

Museo Horne

This eclectic mix of high art and Renaissance and medieval domestic paraphernalia is the personal collection of Englishman Herbert Percy Horne and has been open to the public since 1922. Be sure to check out Giotto's signed *St Stephen* panel, one of the masterpieces in this collection. ❸ Via de' Benci 6 ❶ 055 244 661 ❿ www.museohorne.it ❶ 09.00–13.00 Mon–Sat ❿ Bus: C3, 23, 71 ❶ Admission charge

Museo Nazionale del Bargello (Bargello Museum)

This building has been a prison, a seat of government, a torture chamber and law courts. Its name comes from the title of the 16th-century chief of police. In its current incarnation it holds the national collection of sculpture, most notably Michelangelo's *Bacchus Drunk* and Donatello's two famous sculptures *David* and *St George*. ❸ Via del Proconsolo 4 ❶ 055 238 8606 ❶ 08.15–17.00 Tues–Sat; also open 1st, 3rd & 5th Mon of the month & 2nd & 4th Sun of the month ❿ Bus: C1, C2 ❶ Admission charge

RETAIL THERAPY

Alessandro Bizzarri Come here if you have a headache or other minor ailment for handmade herbal remedies. ⓐ Via della Condotta 32r ⓣ 055 211 580 ⓦ www.bizzarri-fi.biz ⓛ 09.00–13.00 & 15.30–19.00 daily ⓝ Bus: C1, C2, 14

Equoland Spend money and feel good at the same time. Lots of pretty ethnic jewellery and garments as well as Fair Trade chocolate and coffee. ⓐ Via Ghibellina 115r ⓣ 055 264 5700 ⓦ www.equoland.it ⓛ 10.00–13.00 & 14.00–19.30 daily ⓝ Bus: C1, C2, 14

Ethic A little work of art in itself, this sells interesting clothes and books, music and household goods. ⓐ Borgo degli Albizi 37 ⓣ 055 234 4413 ⓦ www.ethic.it ⓛ 10.00–20.00 Tues–Sat, 15.00–20.00 Sun & Mon ⓝ Bus: C1, C2, 14

Mercato di Sant'Ambrogio Tasty picnic food in a smaller and less noisy version of Mercato Centrale. Outside are more domestic stalls – cheap underwear, some second-hand racks for fans of vintage clothes to rummage through, some crockery seconds worth browsing and more. ⓐ Piazza Lorenzo Ghiberti ⓛ 07.00–14.00 Mon–Sat ⓝ Bus: C2, C3, 14

Piazza dei Ciompi Permanent stalls sell everything from genuine antiques to flea-market items. Be sure to browse around the edge of the square as well, as the market is surrounded by loads of fantastic antiques stores. ⓛ 09.00–19.30 daily (Apr–Oct); 09.00–19.30 Tues–Sun (Nov–Mar) ⓝ Bus: C2, C3, 14

Société Anonyme This 'Clothing Concept Store' stocks a range of uniquely different brands, as well as Freitag messenger bags and funky Flygirl shoes. Very friendly staff. 🅐 Via Niccolini 3f, corner of Via della Mattonaia 🅣 055 386 0084 🅦 www.societeanonyme.it 🅛 10.00–14.00 & 15.30–20.00 Mon–Sat 🅝 Bus: C2, C3, 14, 31, 32

Wilma Right in the tourist heart of the city so no big bargains, but good for leather bags and shoes and they do some wacky leather-covered crash helmets. 🅐 Piazza San Firenze 16r 🅣 055 289 087 🅛 12.00–19.30 Mon, 10.00–19.30 Tues–Sat 🅝 Bus: C1, C2

TAKING A BREAK

La Loggia degli Albizi £ ❶ It may not look very exciting from the outside, but the cakes and pastries at this small bar are some of the best in town. 🅐 Borgo degli Albizi 39r 🅣 055 247 9574 🅛 07.30–20.30 Mon–Sat (Sept–July) 🅝 Bus: C1, C2, 14

🔺 *Everyone enjoys a snack break in Piazza della Signoria*

La Loggia del Pesce £ ❷ Stop here for an *aperitivo* under the arched remains of the city's 17th-century fish market. ❸ Piazza dei Ciompi ⏱ 19.00–late daily ⓦ Bus: C2, C3

Moyo £ ❸ Serving everything from breakfast to light lunch to cocktails. Go for the seasonal salads and lunch specials or for the late-night DJs. ❸ Via de' Benci 23r ☎ 055 247 9738 ⓦ www.moyo.it ⏱ 08.30–03.00 daily ⓦ Bus: C3, 23

Rivoire £ ❹ The ultimate place for people-watching in this fascinating square. Waiters in white jackets and bow ties, millions of pounds worth of artwork to gaze at, excellent coffee and good hot chocolate. ❸ Piazza della Signoria 5r ☎ 055 214 412 ⓦ www.rivoire.it ⏱ 08.00–24.00 Tues–Sun (May–Oct); 08.00–20.30 Tues–Sun (Nov–Apr); closed two weeks in Jan ⓦ Bus: C1, C2

🔺 *Rest easy while overlooking the famous view of Florence's skyline*

Rosticceria Giuliano £ ➎ Spit-roast shop selling all manner of cooked and preserved goodies for a picnic; pay a little more to eat at the tables in the back. Right across the road at No 65r is their bar All' Antico Vinaio. ➌ Via dei Neri 74r ➊ 055 238 2723 ➋ 08.00–20.30 Tues–Sat, 08.00–13.00 Sun ➍ Bus: C3, 23

Vivoli £ ➏ Florence's most famous *gelateria*, serving ice cream in a side street close to Santa Croce church. ➌ Via Isola delle Stinche 7, off Via Bentaccordi ➊ 055 292 334 ➍ www.vivoli.it ➋ 07.30–24.00 Tues–Sat, 09.30–01.00 Sun (Sept–July) ➍ Bus: C2, C3, 14

'Ino £–££ ➐ Tucked away behind the Uffizi, this contemporary deli is a great place for a delicious *panino* (warm sandwich), made to order from quality ingredients. It's also good for foodie gifts. ➌ Via de' Georgofili 3r–7r, near Uffizi ➊ 055 219 208 ➍ www.ino-firenze.com ➋ 11.00–17.00 daily ➍ Bus: C1, C2

AFTER DARK

RESTAURANTS

Darvish Café £ ➑ For a break from traditional Tuscan cuisine, head to Darvish Café for Greek and Arab dishes or one of their Persian teas. Vegetarian options are available and between 16.00 and 19.00 the restaurant offers two-for-one on anything ordered. ➌ Via Ghibellina 76r ➊ 055 390 0742 ➋ 10.00–late daily ➍ Bus: C2, C3, 14

Il Pizzaiuolo £–££ ➒ Quality Neapolitan pizzas – the kind with the thicker base – in this rather bare but very popular place. ➌ Via de' Macci 113r ➊ 055 241 171 ➋ 12.30–15.00 & 19.30–00.30 daily ➍ Bus: C2, C3, 14

Rex Café £–££ ❿ A good place for an *aperitivo* and tapas-like snacks, vibrant, mosaic-decorated Rex has music and dancing into the small hours. ❸ Via Fiesolana 25r ❶ 055 248 0331 ❶ 17.00–02.30 daily (Sept–May) ❷ Bus: C1, 14, 23

Boccanegra £–£££ ⓫ Two restaurants, side by side. The main restaurant is classy and innovative, with all the usual meat and fish dishes and an excellent wine list. Next door is for pizza. Specify which restaurant you would like when booking. ❸ Via Ghibellina 124r ❶ 055 200 1098 ❾ www.boccanegra.com ❶ 19.00–24.00 Mon–Sat ❷ Bus: C2, C3, 14

Coquinarius ££ ⓬ Possibly the best-value eaterie in this part of the city. Traditional Tuscan food – hare sauce, octopus carpaccio, pear and cheese ravioli. Good for vegetarians as well as carnivores. ❸ Via delle Oche 15r, off Via de' Tosinghi ❶ 055 230 2153 ❶ 12.00–23.00 Mon–Thur, 12.00–23.30 Fri & Sat; closed three weeks in Aug ❷ Bus: C1, C2

Cibrèo £££ ⓭ Huge reputation among locals but also draws in the tourists. The dessert menu is excellent. Advisable to book. ❸ Via Andrea del Verrochio 5r, off Piazza Lorenzo Ghiberti ❶ 055 234 5853 ❶ 08.00–01.00 Tues–Sat ❷ Bus: C2, C3, 14

Frescobaldi £££ ⓮ A warren of deep red, grey and umber rooms link this classy restaurant and wine bar. Spend the evening over a meal or snack on tapas or cheese plates in the wine bar. Vegetarians will do well here. ❸ Via dei Magazzini 2–4r, off Via della Condotta ❶ 055 284 724 ❾ www.frescobaldi.it ❶ 19.00–22.30 Mon, 12.00–14.30 & 19.00–22.30 Tues–Sat ❷ Bus: C1, C2

Ristorante Il Caminetto £££ ⓯ Aimed at the tourist trade with menus in English and a very attractive seating area outside. In a quiet square behind the Duomo, this is ideal for a posh night out. Simple dishes are cooked well and if the garden seating doesn't appeal, the interior is just as attractively laid out. ⓐ Via dello Studio 34r ⓣ 055 239 6274 ⓦ www.ilcaminettofirenze.it ⓛ 12.00–15.00 & 19.00–23.00 Thur–Tues ⓝ Bus: C1, C2, 14

BARS & CLUBS

Jazz Club Long-established basement club with live music most nights. ⓐ Via Nuova de' Caccini 3 ⓣ 055 247 9700 ⓦ www.jazzclubfirenze.com ⓛ 21.00–late Tues–Sat (Sept–Jun) ⓝ Bus: C1, 14

I Visacci This deeply cool wine bar will appeal to the young and arty. Bright colours, Latin American music every night, aperitifs from 18.30 and good food. ⓐ Borgo degli Albizi 8or ⓣ 055 200 1956 ⓛ 10.00–03.00 daily ⓝ Bus: C1, C2, 14, 23

ARTS & ENTERTAINMENT

Zuberteatro has been organising *Fiume Arno spettacoli in barca* (theatrical performances on boats floating along the Arno) since 1999. Take a peek from the riverbanks or from bridges, or you can get on the boats at Porticciola in Piazza Mentana. The same group also performs *Villa Fabbricotti spettacoli nel verde*, which is theatre in the park. ⓐ Parco di Villa Fabbricotti, Via Vittorio Emanuele II 64 ⓣ 055 500 0640 ⓦ www.zauberteatro.com

Piazza della Repubblica & around

This part of the city is dominated by the two piazzas, Repubblica and Santa Maria Novella. The chief attraction here is shopping, with all the big designer names and lots of small boutiques touting clothes, household goods and, most of all, shoes.

This is also the part of the city which you are likely to encounter in your first few minutes in Florence. The train and bus station can be a scary place for new arrivals but the taxi rank at the front of the station will get you to your hotel and the tourist office inside the station provides help, accommodation and maps.

The bustling city centre is easily navigable on foot. Should you need public transport to access the area, hop on Bus C1 or C2, which serve the area well.

SIGHTS & ATTRACTIONS

Mercato Nuovo

Mercato Nuovo means 'New Market' – in this case 'new' means 16th century. A market has been here since the 11th century, though the current building is a mere 400 years old. In Florence it is obligatory to have your photo taken here with *Il Porcellino*, the famous bronze boar statue. The fountain dates from the 17th century and its original, carved out of Roman marble, is in the Uffizi. In the evening the market is a pleasant place to watch the buskers. ❸ Off Via Calimala ❶ 09.00–19.00 daily (Apr–Oct); 09.00–19.00 Tues–Sat (Nov–Mar) Ⓝ Bus: C1, C2

Ognissanti (Church of All Saints)

The Church of All Saints was the family church of the explorer Amerigo Vespucci, who gave his name to the landmass that

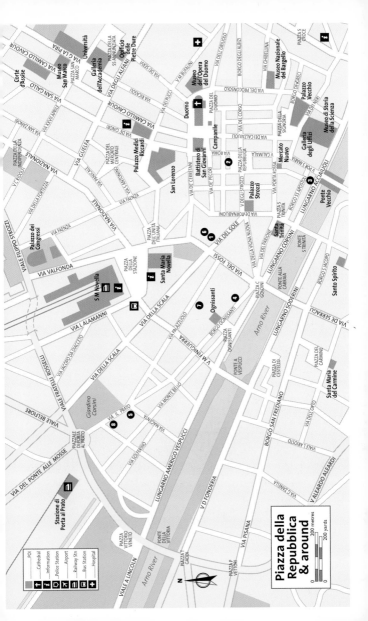

◐ *Florence's famous bronze boar,* Il Porcellino

Columbus had discovered. The new continent and the young Amerigo are portrayed in the *Madonna della Misericordia* by Ghirlandaio inside the church. In the adjoining refectory is Ghirlandaio's *Last Supper*. Botticelli is buried here and the church also contains his fresco *St Augustine*. Visit early in the morning when the monks are gliding about to the sound of choral music. ➌ Borgo Ognissanti 42 ➊ 055 239 8700 ⏰ 07.30–12.30 & 15.30–19.30 daily, *Last Supper* 09.00–12.00 Mon, Tues & Sat ⏹ Bus: C3, D

Palazzo Strozzi

A beautiful building designed by architect Benedetto da Maiano for early 16th-century banker Filippo Strozzi. Stop in to see the sun-dappled courtyard, or check out one of the temporary exhibitions staged by the Fondazione Strozzi. ➌ Piazza Strozzi ➊ 055 277 6461 ⓦ www.palazzostrozzi.org ⏹ Bus: C1, 6, 36, 37

Santa Trinità

Originally a simple 11th-century church, this place became more ornate as the centuries passed and the monastic order which built it adjusted their vows of poverty to their increasing wealth. The interesting features are Ghirlandaio's 15th-century frescoes, which actually portray local figures of the time – the Medici's bank manager, Francesco Sassetti and his wife, Ghirlandaio himself (as the first dark-haired shepherd in the nativity scene), Lorenzo de Medici and various family members. In one scene St Francis is portrayed in Piazza Santa Trinità, allowing a peek at what the square looked like during the 15th century. ➌ Piazza Santa Trinità ➊ 055 216 912 ⏰ 08.00–12.00 & 16.00–18.00 Mon–Sat, 16.00–18.00 Sun ⏹ Bus: C3, 36, 37

PONTE VECCHIO (OLD BRIDGE)

The Arno River has been spanned by a bridge at this point since the Romans first settled here in 59 BC. The current structure dates back to the 14th century and was one of the few bridges to escape destruction by the retreating German army during World War II. Originally filled with tanners and butchers, it has been the home of goldsmiths and jewellers since 1593.

Today the bridge is lined on both sides by shops, some of which have extensions hanging over the water. You will notice lots of padlocks locked on to iron rings set in the walls of the bridge. Lovers fix the padlocks and throw the keys into the river as a sign of their enduring love.

A passage known as the Vasari corridor links the Palazzo Vecchio on the north side with the Palazzo Pitti on the south. It was built to allow the Medici to travel from one of their palaces to the other without coming into contact with the general public.

During the day the bridge is a lively place. The shops offer everything from junk earrings to classy antiques, but there are few bargains. Just enjoy the atmosphere of it all.

CULTURE

Museo di Santa Maria Novella

The old cloisters of the monastery of Santa Maria Novella (see page 77) have been converted into a museum. On display here are the frescoes in the chapel used by the Spanish family members of Cosimo I's wife.

They depict more salvation and damnation, featuring the Dominicans themselves as the hounds of the Lord (*domini canes* in Latin – a play on the name Dominican), saving souls and punishing those who will not be saved. The frescoes are by Andrea di Firenze. ⓐ Piazza Santa Maria Novella ⓣ 055 282 187 ⓞ 09.00–17.00 Mon–Thur & Sat ⓝ Bus: D, 36, 37 ⓘ Admission charge

Santa Maria Novella

This former monastery was built by the Dominicans in the 13th century. The exterior was given a 15th-century facelift and extension, paid for by the merchant family Rucellai, whose name modestly appears on the upper storey. Inside, note the way that the length of the church is given an apparent extension by the line of columns which were built closer and lower as they approach the altar.

What draws the visitor into this church, though, are its decorations. Look out for Masaccio's fresco *Trinity*, which must have astonished the 15th-century congregation with its innovative use of perspective, for Giotto's *Crucifix* of 1288, and for Filippo Lippi's 15th-century cycle of frescoes in the little chapel to the right of the chancel.

Around the altar, Ghirlandaio created a series of frescoes of scenes from the New Testament that say more about 15th-century life than they do about the birth of the Virgin Mary or John the Baptist. If you haven't used up all your fresco appreciation by now, look in the Cappella Strozzi at the end of the left transept, which contains frescoes by Nardi di Cione that are probably his masterpiece. The people who paid for the painting are shown being led into heaven by St Michael, while those who missed out on (or couldn't pay for) penance are seen being shovelled into hell. ⓐ Piazza Santa Maria Novella ⓣ 055 219 257 ⓞ 09.30–17.30 Mon–Thur, 11.00–17.00 Fri, 09.00–17.00 Sat, 13.00–17.00 Sun ⓝ Bus: D, 36, 37 ⓘ Admission charge

RETAIL THERAPY

This part of the city attracts serious shoppers. Via de' Tornabuoni
is designer heaven. Look out for **Ferragamo** at No 2r, **Emilio Pucci**
at No 20r, **Armani** at Nos 48–50, **Gucci** at No 73r, **Prada** at No 67r,
Versace at Nos 13–15, **Bulgari** at No 61r and **Parenti** at No 67r.
For lesser-known but more affordable boutiques, Via della
Vigna Nuova, Via Porta Rossa and Via Roma are full of tiny
shops. Ponte Vecchio is the home of jewellers. The following are
a tiny sample.

BM Bookshop Far off the average shopper's beaten path, this
small shop has a varied selection of English-language books
on Florence, Tuscany and Italy, as well as truly vintage
cookbooks and novels. ⓐ Borgo Ognissanti 4r ⓣ 055 294 575
ⓔ bmbookshop@dada.it ⓛ 09.30–19.30 Mon–Sat
ⓝ Bus: C3, 36, 37

Emilio Cavallini Tiny shop with T-shirts, underwear and matching
tights, tops and socks, all in original prints. ⓐ Via della Vigna
Nuova 24r ⓣ 055 238 2789 ⓦ www.emiliocavallini.com
ⓛ 15.00–19.00 Mon, 10.00–19.00 Tues–Sat ⓝ Bus: C3, 6, 36, 37

Eredi Chiarini Italian men's clothes, classic and elegant.
ⓐ Via Roma 16r ⓣ 055 284 4781 ⓦ www.eredichiarini.com
ⓛ 15.30–19.30 Mon, 10.00–19.30 Tues–Sat ⓝ Bus: C1, C2

Farmacia Santa Maria Novella The most luxurious soap ever,
on sale in an ancient pharmacy. ⓐ Via della Scala 16 ⓣ 055 216 276
ⓦ www.smnovella.it ⓛ 09.30–19.30 daily ⓝ Bus: 36, 37

Furla Beautiful bags, shoes, watches and belts in respectable plain leather or crazy patterns. ⓐ Via della Vigna Nuova 47r ⓣ 055 282 779 ⓦ www.furla.com ⓛ 10.00–19.30 Mon–Sat, 11.00–19.00 Sun ⓝ Bus: C3, 6, 36, 37

Mercato Nuovo Home of the bronze boar, whose nose you must rub if you wish to return to the city, this place sells plastic Davids, Duomos, comedy aprons, bags, belts, scarves, costume jewellery – plenty of potential gifts for the family. ⓐ Off Via Calimala ⓛ 09.00–19.00 daily (Apr–Oct); 09.00–19.00 Tues–Sat (Nov–Mar) ⓝ Bus: C1, C2

Miu Miu For those who can't afford Prada, here are their younger, less expensive clothes. ⓐ Via Roma 8r ⓣ 055 260 8931 ⓦ www.miumiu.com ⓛ 10.00–19.00 daily ⓝ Bus: C1, C2

Raspini Vintage If you can't afford the Armani or Prada in the Raspini shop in Via Roma, come here for last year's collection at almost affordable prices. ⓐ Via Calimaruzza 17r ⓣ 055 213 901 ⓛ 10.30–19.30 Tues–Sat, 15.30–19.30 Sun & Mon ⓝ Bus: C1, C2

Rinascente Lovely department store in the old-fashioned sense, with designer concessions, lingerie, beautiful linens and a rooftop café with views. ⓐ Piazza della Repubblica 1 ⓣ 055 219 113 ⓦ www.rinascente.it ⓛ 09.00–21.00 Mon–Sat, 10.30–20.00 Sun ⓝ Bus: C1, C2

Le Stanze Funky home furnishings and kitchen objects. Pick up a set of Buddha jelly moulds, or a pad of paper placemats. ⓐ Borgo Ognissanti 50–52r ⓣ 055 288 921 ⓛ 10.30–19.30 Tues–Sat ⓝ Bus: C3, 36, 37

TAKING A BREAK

Piazza della Repubblica is the place to people-watch and there are some good cafés in which to position yourself. Along Via della Spada are several good places to buy picnic food – try Franco Moreno at 46r (🕐 08.00–13.00 & 17.00–19.30 daily), while almost opposite is Panificio, a bakery (🕐 07.45–13.00 & 17.00–19.30 daily).

Forno Top £ ❶ Good bakery close to the station. Lovely cakes, focaccia bread and sandwiches. 🅰 Via della Spada 23r, off Via del Sole 🕿 055 212 461 🕐 07.30–13.30 & 17.00–19.30 Mon–Sat, closes early Wed 🚍 Bus: C1, 6, 36, 37

Caffè Gilli ££ ❷ Great for people-watching, this Florentine institution is gloriously decorated inside and has a large garden of potted plants in the square. 🅰 Piazza della Repubblica 1 🕿 055 213 896 🌐 www.gilli.it 🕐 07.30–23.00 daily 🚍 Bus: C1, C2

The Fusion Bar – Gallery Hotel Art ££ ❸ Stop for a swish *aperitivo* near the end of Ponte Vecchio. Trendy and upmarket venue, with prices to match. 🅰 Vicolo dell'Oro 5, off Lungarno Acciaiuoli 🕿 055 27 263 🌐 www.lungarnohotels.com 🚍 Bus: C1, C2

Sei Divino ££ ❹ Snack on tasty nibbles against a background of jazzy tunes during happy hour. 🅰 Borgo Ognissanti 42r 🕿 055 217 791 🕐 12.00–22.30 daily 🚍 Bus: C3, 36, 37

AFTER DARK

RESTAURANTS

Funiculi £ ❺ Enormous restaurant serving excellent pizzas and other dishes based on ingredients sourced in Naples. ⓐ Via Il Prato 81r ❶ 055 264 6553 ⓛ 12.00–15.00 & 19.00–01.00 Mon–Fri, 19.00–01.00 Sat & Sun ⓝ Bus: C2, C3, 12, 13

Rosticceria della Spada £–££ ❻ Traditional Tuscan food to eat in or take away. The dining room is plain and unfussy and there is a good inexpensive set menu for lunch and dinner. Takeaway costs about half. ⓐ Via della Spade 62r, off Via del Sole ❶ 055 218 757 ⓦ www.laspadaitalia.com ⓛ 12.00–15.00 & 18.00–22.30 daily ⓝ Bus: C1, 36, 37

Osteria dei Cento Poveri £££ ❼ In a quiet backstreet behind Santa Maria Novella, this little gem of a restaurant serves great fish – try the sea bass, sea bream or lobster gnocchi. ⓐ Via Palazzuolo 31r ❶ 055 218 846 ⓦ www.centopoveri.it ⓛ 12.00–15.00 & 19.00–24.00 daily ⓝ Bus: C2, 36, 37

BARS & CLUBS

Officina Move Bar £ ❽ Trendy bar serving quick breakfasts and café lunches with a changing daily menu of pizzas, pastas and salads. At night it reinvents itself as a disco bar with cocktails and *aperitivos* at 19.30, followed by all kinds of music, occasionally live. ⓐ Via Il Prato 58r ❶ 055 210 399 ⓛ 08.00–02.00 Mon–Fri, 18.30–03.00 Sat & Sun (Sept–July) ⓝ Bus: C2, C3, 12, 13

The Duomo & north

You could happily spend several days sightseeing in this area to the north of the city centre. All roads seem to lead to the Duomo and it is visible from across the city. North of it is the Accademia, and north again is Museo San Marco, one of the finest small museums in the city. San Lorenzo is another big draw, as is its museum, which displays statues by Michelangelo. The market stalls around San Lorenzo and the Mercato Centrale are also good.

Again, it's best to wander around the Duomo on foot. Now that the square is closed to traffic, it's a much more pleasant experience to wander around the area. Should you need to use public transport, hop on Bus C1, 14 or 23.

SIGHTS & ATTRACTIONS

Battistero di San Giovanni (Baptistery)

This tiny octagonal church, dedicated to St John the Baptist, was built in the 11th century. Highlights of the church include amazing mosaics decorating the domed ceiling, which represent the Last Judgement and the mouth of hell.

The bronze doors of the church are also fascinating. The south doors, cast in the 1330s by Andrea Pisano, depict the life of John the Baptist. The north doors, commissioned in 1401 and made by Lorenzo Ghiberti, tell the story of Christ. The same artist also made the staggeringly beautiful east doors in 1424–54, depicting stories from the Old Testament. Called by Michelangelo 'The Gates of Paradise', the originals are safely stowed away in the Museo dell'Opera del Duomo (see page 92). Experts consider these panels to be the first indication of the Renaissance period in art, with their focus on

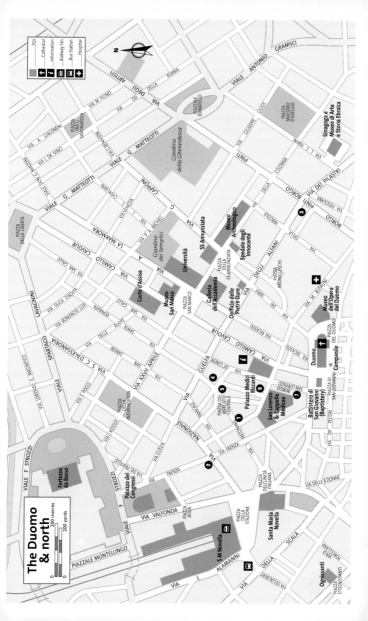

◢ *The Duomo*

lifelike figures and sense of perspective. Incidentally, you can see Ghiberti in the bronze door frame itself – his is the fourth head down on the right-hand side. ⓐ Piazza di San Giovanni ⓦ www.operaduomo.firenze.it ⓛ 12.00–19.00 Mon–Sat, 08.30–14.00 Sun Ⓝ Bus: C1, C2, 14, 23 ⓘ Admission charge

Duomo (Cathedral)

The Duomo dominates the Florentine skyline. More than 600 years have passed since its construction began, yet it is still the biggest masonry dome in the world. The cathedral is actually called Santa Maria del Fiore, taking its name from the symbolic white flower which the Angel Gabriel gave to the Virgin Mary, representing the Immaculate Conception.

Between 1296 and 1436, when the dome was finally completed, four generations of architects dedicated their lives to building the cathedral. The real sight is the exterior, with its three colours of marble inlaid in patterns. Most of the exterior is actually now a 19th-century reconstruction, but the south side remains original. The dome itself, accessed from outside the cathedral, can be climbed for incredible views over the city. It's a stiff climb and not for the claustrophobic or faint of heart.

The interior is positively austere compared to the decadence outside. The inside of the dome contains frescoes of hell and the Last Judgement, painstakingly painted on to the wet plaster by Vasari and Federico Zucchari. The frescoes include images of many of the city's most notable characters of the time.

You can visit the crypt, which contains the remains of Santa Reparata, the 4th-century church that stood here before the Duomo. There are Roman remains here as well. Brunelleschi, the man who finally achieved the monumental task of finishing the roof, is buried here.

Beside the cathedral is its 14th-century bell tower, the **Campanile**, built by an assortment of famous names – Giotto, Pisano and Francesco Talenti. This last, lesser-known architect was responsible for thickening the walls at the base of the Campanile, thus avoiding another leaning tower situation. A climb to the top is easier than climbing the Duomo and gives pleasant views over the city and of the dome itself.

Duomo & Santa Reparata ⓐ Piazza del Duomo ⓣ 055 230 2885 ⓦ www.operaduomo.firenze.it ⓛ 10.00–17.00 Mon–Wed & Fri, 10.00–15.30 Thur, 10.00–16.45 Sat, 13.30–16.45 Sun; closes at 15.30 first Sat of the month ⓥ Bus: C1, C2, 14, 23 ⓘ Separate admission charges for Duomo and Santa Reparata

Cupola (Dome) ⓛ 08.30–19.00 Mon–Fri, 08.30–17.40 Sat ⓘ Closes at 16.00 first Sat of the month ⓘ Admission charge

Campanile ⓛ 08.30–19.30 daily ⓘ Admission charge

THE BIGGEST DOME IN THE WORLD

In medieval times, domes were built using the Roman technique of creating a wooden shell and building around it. The shell supported the bricks until the dome was complete and the bricks could hold themselves in place.

The Duomo's dome, however, was to be so big that no wooden structure could support it. The problem was solved by building two shells of stone beams and by filling each with a herringbone pattern of bricks.

It took 16 years to build the dome. Workers stayed up there all day, eating their lunch where they worked to save the 40-minute climb down and then up again.

Giardino dei Semplici

Originally owned by Dominican nuns, this 2-hectare (5-acre) plot
was seized by Cosimo I in order to create a physic garden. Pisa and
Padua had physic gardens, so the Medici had to have one too. The
garden still grows medicinal herbs, as it did under Cosimo, but it has
now also become the city's botanic gardens and tropical plants have
been added to the herbs.

At the entrance to the garden is the **Museo di Geologia e
Paleontologia** (Museum of Geology and Palaeontology), full
of bones and fossils, which make a nice change from all the
displays of elaborate art and furnishings in the other
museums and churches.

Giardino dei Semplici ❷ Via Per Antonio Micheli 3 ❶ 055 275 7402
🕐 09.00–13.00 Tues–Fri (June–Sept); 09.00–13.00 Mon–Fri
(Oct–May) ❶ Admission charge

Museo di Geologia ❶ 055 275 7536 🕐 10.00–13.00 Mon, Fri & Sun,
10.00–13.00 & 16.00–19.00 Tues & Thur, 10.00–18.00 Sat Ⓝ Bus: C1,
14, 17, 23

Palazzo Medici Riccardi

This palace is yet another of those owned by the Medici. It has been
turned into government offices but parts of it are open to the public.
It is worth seeing the Gozzoli frescoes, ostensibly representing the
journey of the Magi but in reality glorifying the Medici name by
depicting them as the Three Kings. Individual Medici can be made
out in the frescoes, notably Lorenzo the Magnificent on a grey horse
at a distance from the rest of the procession. On the first floor of the
building is a *Madonna and Child* by Filippo Lippi and in the gallery
there is another ceiling fresco representing the ascent into heaven
of the entire Medici family. As you enter the building, admire the

windows on either side of the entrance, which were designed by Michelangelo. ❷ Via Camillo Cavour 1 ☎ 055 276 0340 ⏰ 09.00–19.00 Thur–Tues ❺ Bus: C1, 14, 23 ❶ Book ahead in high summer or if there is an exhibition ❶ Admission charge

San Lorenzo

This ancient church, designed by Brunelleschi and paid for by the godfather of the Medici clan, Giovanni di Bicci de Medici, was never completed, as the bare bricks on the façade indicate. Giovanni ran out of money and although his son Cosimo put up some more to complete the interior, plans for the exterior never saw fruition.

There is much to look out for in the church. The bronze pulpits and doors of the Old Sacristy are by Donatello, while Filippo Lippi painted an Annunciation in the north transept. On the north wall of the church is the tortured *Martyrdom of St Lawrence* by Bronzino.

Generations of the Medici are buried in the side chapels of this church. Cosimo's tomb, in the centre of the church, is modestly labelled *Pater Patriae* (Father of the Fatherland). More Medici are in the Sagrestia Vecchia. Giovanni is here with two of his grandsons, amid beautiful decorations by Donatello.

There is a charge to see the rest of the Medici funerary ornaments, which are made by Michelangelo. The **Cappelle Medicee** is entered from Piazza Madonna degli Aldobrandini. Beyond some minor Medici family members in the crypt, and the later royal Medici in the Chapel of the Princes, you come to the Sagrestia Nuova and the tombs designed and carved by Michelangelo. He portrays two Medici men with contrasting characters. Lorenzo, Duke of Urbino, is depicted as a philosopher, while the other, Giuliano, Duke of Nemours, is an action man. Opposite them is the uncompleted *Madonna and Child*, finished off by Michelangelo's assistants.

Next door to the church is the **Biblioteca Medicea-Laurenziana**, designed by Michelangelo to hold the Medici collection of important papers and books. The vestibule is open to the public although the reading room itself may not be. The staircase, in a style now called mannerism, has wavy steps flowing down into the room while the walls are decorated with empty niches and disappearing columns that are not designed to support anything.

Church ❸ Piazza San Lorenzo ❶ 055 216 634 ● 10.00–17.00 Mon–Sat
Ⓝ Bus: C1, 36, 37 ❶ Admission charge
Cappelle (Side chapels) ● 08.30–17.00 Tues–Sat, 08.30–13.50 Sun
❶ Admission charge
Biblioteca ● 08.30–13.30 Mon–Sat

Santissima Annunziata

This church, built in the 15th century, contains a painting begun in 1252 by one of the monks and allegedly finished off by an angel while he slept. The portico contains frescoes by Andrea del Sarto and others but was damaged in the flood of 1966. Traditionally, Florentine newlyweds come here to lay a bouquet by the Virgin to ask for a fruitful marriage. Above the entrance porch to the Chiostro dei Morti (Cloister of the Dead), which is full of memorial tablets, is del Sarto's *La Madonna del Sacco*. ❸ Piazza della Santissima Annunziata ❶ 055 266 181 ● 07.30–12.30 & 16.00–18.30 daily
Ⓝ Bus: C1, 6, 14, 23

Spedale degli Innocente (Hospital of the Innocents)

The first orphanage in Europe, this building, designed by Brunelleschi and opened in 1419, was commissioned by the silk weavers' guild. It took in unwanted children, who were placed on the rotating stone at the left of the *loggia*.

The museum upstairs contains a little cache of Renaissance art including an *Adoration of the Magi* by Domenico Ghirlandaio. Outside, check out the piazza with its two wacky mannerist fountains by Pietro Tacca. If you are in Florence on 25 March, the Feast of the Annunciation, come here to see the fair. 🅐 Piazza della Santissima Annunziata 12 🕔 055 203 7308 🕔 10.00–19.00 daily 🅝 Bus: C1, 6, 14, 23 🅘 Admission charge

CULTURE

Galleria dell'Accademia (Accademia Gallery)

Home to Michelangelo's *David*, this is one of Florence's biggest draws. If you can, visit the Bargello (see page 65) to see other representations of David, the youth who kills the powerful warrior Goliath, before coming to see this. The figure stood for hundreds of years out in the open in Piazza della Signoria but is now safely protected in here. The other statues in here by Michelangelo are all unfinished and it is fascinating to see the great man's work in progress. 🅐 Via Ricasoli 58–60 🕔 055 238 8609 🕔 08.15–18.50 Tues–Sun 🅝 Bus: C1, 14, 23 🅘 Admission charge

Museo Archeologico (Archaeology Museum)

In all this surfeit of Renaissance and medieval art it is easy to forget that Florence was once Roman and before that Etruscan. This museum remedies that by concentrating on displays of Etruscan and Roman art. There are also exhibits of Egyptian and Greek artefacts. 🅐 Piazza della Santissima Annunziata 9b 🕔 055 23575 🅦 www.archeotoscana.beniculturali.it 🕔 08.00–19.00 Tues–Fri, 08.00–14.00 Sat & Sun 🅝 Bus: C1, 14, 23 🅘 Admission charge

⬤ *To see Michelangelo's David is some people's sole reason for visiting Florence*

Museo dell'Opera del Duomo

The highlight of this museum, which is filled with beautiful works of art, is Michelangelo's *Pietà*, carved in the artist's final years and intended for his tomb. Raging with frustration one day the artist smashed Christ's leg but the sculpture was successfully repaired by his assistants. On the upper floors look out for life-sized figures carved by Donatello. ⓐ Piazza del Duomo 9 ⓣ 055 230 2885 ⓦ www.operaduomo.firenze.it ⓛ 09.00–19.30 Mon–Sat, 09.00–13.45 Sun ⓝ Bus: C1, C2, 14, 23 ⓘ Admission charge

Museo San Marco

The former monastery of the Dominican order of San Marco is now a museum largely dedicated to the work of Fra Angelico, a brother and later the prior of the monastery. In the downstairs rooms are works by Fra Angelico, Ghirlandaio and others. Many of them are copies, showing how artists sometimes churned out paintings to order. Fra Bartolomeo's portrait of Savonarola, who lived here for a time and whose rooms upstairs contain fragments of his clothes and possessions, depicts him as a fundamentalist figure.

The cells upstairs are the biggest reason to visit here. Painted by Fra Angelico and his assistants, each room contains a little sacred fresco. At the top of the stairs is one of the most breathtaking paintings in Florence – Angelico's *Annunciation*. ⓐ Piazza San Marco 1 ⓣ 055 238 8608 ⓦ www.polomuseale.firenze.it ⓛ 08.15–13.50 Tues–Fri, 1st, 3rd & 5th Mon of the month, 2nd & 4th Sun of the month, 08.15–16.50 Sat ⓝ Bus: C1, 14, 23 ⓘ Admission charge

Opificio delle Pietre Dure

A museum depicting the making of mosaics. The museum not only has exhibits of tools and methods, but actually restores ancient mosaics. Make an appointment to watch the restoration work under way. ⓐ Via degli Alfani 78 ⓘ 055 218 709 ⓛ 08.15–14.00 Mon, Wed, Fri & Sat, 08.15–19.00 Thur ⓝ Bus: C1 ⓘ Admission charge

Sinagoga e Museo di Arte e Storia Ebraica (Synagogue & Museum of Jewish Art and History)

An elaborate 19th-century synagogue with a museum telling the history of Jews in Florence. ⓐ Via Farini 4 ⓘ 055 234 6654 ⓛ 10.00–17.00 Sun–Thur (Apr–Sept); 10.00–15.00 Sun–Thur, 10.00–14.00 Fri (Nov–Mar) ⓝ Bus: C1, 6, 31, 32 ⓘ Admission charge

RETAIL THERAPY

Borgo San Lorenzo This street, which runs north from Piazza di San Giovanni, is filled with cafés and small boutiques selling inexpensive clothes. There are lots of handbag shops as well as more ordinary chains. ⓝ Bus: C1, C2

Collections Alice Atelier The strangest *commedia dell'arte* masks you ever saw – leaf masks, daisy masks, Pinocchio masks, wooden puppets, carvings and more. ⓐ Via Faenza 72r ⓘ 055 287 370 ⓦ www.alicemasks.com ⓛ 09.00–13.00 & 15.30–19.30 Mon–Sat ⓝ Bus: 4

Falsi Gioielli Handmade bead, plastic and resin jewellery – they may not be expensive stones but they are certainly gems. ⓐ Via de' Ginori 34r ⓘ 055 287 237 ⓛ 10.00–19.30 Mon–Fri, 10.00–14.00 Sat ⓝ Bus: C1, 14, 23

◗ *Buy fresh produce from the bustling Mercato Centrale*

Mercato Centrale The biggest fresh-food market in the city, this one is good for picnic food, watching Florentines at work and for the many souvenir and clothes stalls around the square. The market is usually on only in the mornings, but one or two of the restaurants serving market workers are open all night. ⓐ Piazza del Mercato Centrale ⏰ 07.00–14.00 Mon–Sat (summer); 07.00–14.00 Mon–Fri, 16.00–20.00 Sat (winter) Ⓝ Bus: C1, 14, 23

Il Papiro Classic paper-products shop with beautiful handmade notebooks, Christmas cards and other goodies. ⓐ Piazza del Duomo 24r ⓣ 055 281 628 Ⓦ www.ilpapirofirenze.it ⏰ 10.00–13.00 & 14.00–19.00 daily Ⓝ Bus: C1, C2

San Lorenzo Market Hundreds of stalls surround San Lorenzo church. You can stock up on gifts to take home for the family, add to your handbag collection with a good fake designer handbag or splash out on a leather coat. ⏰ 09.00–19.00 daily Ⓝ Bus: C1, 14, 23

TAKING A BREAK

Antica Pasticceria Sieni £ ❶ Glorious pastry shop with pasta and salads for a healthier option. ⓐ Via de Ariento 27r, off Via Panicale ⏰ 08.00–19.00 Tues–Sun Ⓝ Bus: C1, 14, 23

La Lampara £ ❷ Brush past the multilingual menu in the window, pass the logs stacked up for the pizza oven, ignore the indoor tables and head out to the pretty courtyard garden. Good inexpensive food, traditional dishes and popular with locals. ⓐ Via Nazionale 36r ⓣ 055 215 164 ⏰ 12.00–23.30 daily Ⓝ Bus: C1, 14, 23

La Latteria £ ❸ This vegetarian and vegan health-food bar
uses only organic ingredients and serves brunch all day. Try their
speciality *torta di breton*, or milk cake. It's cheaper to sit at the bar.
ⓐ Via degli Alfani 39r ❶ 055 247 8878 ● 08.00–22.00 daily
Ⓝ Bus: C1

Trattoria Mario £–££ ❹ In business since 1953, this excellent
trattoria doesn't take reservations and there are queues out the
door. Go early to get one of the wooden booths. Open for lunch
only. ⓐ Via Rosina 2r, off Piazza del Mercato Centrale ❶ 055 218 550
Ⓦ www.trattoriamario.com ● 12.00–15.30 Mon–Sat (Sept–July)
Ⓝ Bus: C1, 14, 23

AFTER DARK

RESTAURANTS

Da Garibardi £–££ ❺ Located near the San Lorenzo Market,
Da Garibardi serves good cheap *cucina casalinga*, or home-cooked
food. Order an excellent pizza on their large outdoor terrace.
ⓐ Piazza del Mercato Centrale 38r ❶ 055 212 267 Ⓦ www.garibardi.it
● 11.30–23.00 daily Ⓝ Bus: C1, 14, 23

Da Sergio £–££ ❻ Almost hidden by market stalls, this family-run
trattoria has an air of Old Florence. It's a great place to sample local
authentic home cooking with dishes such as *ribollita* (bean and
vegetable soup), *bistecca* (steak), *trippa* (tripe) and *seppie in
inzimino*, a sweet stew of cuttlefish and Swiss chard (on Fridays).
ⓐ Piazza San Lorenzo 8r ❶ 055 281 941 ● 12.00–15.00 Mon–Sat
Ⓝ Bus: C1, 14, 23

Nuti ££ ❼ Two restaurants, one a *pizzeria* and the other a *trattoria*. Very popular and fills up at lunch and dinner. ⓐ Borgo San Lorenzo 22–24r ❶ 055 210 145 ◔ 11.30–01.00 daily ⓝ Bus: C1, 14, 23

BARS & CLUBS

Astor Café The opposite of historical, art-filled Florence, the Astor is loud, shiny and new. Good food during the day, followed by cocktails and live music and DJ sessions downstairs in the evening. ⓐ Piazza del Duomo 20r ❶ 055 239 9318 ◔ 12.30–03.00 daily ⓝ Bus: C1, C2, 14, 23

The Fish Pub Blast the night away with special deals on beer and liqueur shots at this Scottish-themed pub. Happy hour from 16.00 to 20.00. Pick up a flyer for a free drink. Women get free drinks all night on Mondays. ⓐ Piazza del Mercato Centrale 44r ◔ 10.00–02.00 daily ⓝ Bus: C1, 14, 23

Porfirio Rubirosa Named after a Brazilian playboy and lying outside the traffic-restricted city centre, this cool bar is popular in the evenings and weekends when car-driving locals flood in for cocktails, sushi and nightcaps. There's a big alfresco terrace too. ⓐ Viale Filippo Strozzi 38r ❶ 055 490 965 ◔ 09.00–02.00 Mon–Sat ⓝ Bus: 1, 8, 12, 13, 17

Oltrarno

The area of the city that lies south of the Arno has a rural feel, with
the huge Bóboli Gardens and smaller, quieter squares. The little
artisan shops are gradually giving way to elegant restaurants and
expensive shops but there are still lots of sights to see. Over to the
west is the must-see church of Santo Spirito, while Palazzo Pitti's
extravagance will astound you as will the art by Raphael and Titian
within. To the east is Piazzale Michelangelo, which is often crowded
but nonetheless stunning. Set off as dusk falls and be at the Piazzale
in time for an amazing sunset.

It's easiest to access the Oltrarno on foot, with its winding,
narrow roads and pedestrianised squares. Should you need to use
public transport to arrive in the area, hop on Bus C3 or D.

SIGHTS & ATTRACTIONS

Giardino di Bóboli (Bóboli Gardens)

This former sandstone quarry was developed in 1550 into ornate
gardens with clipped box hedges, an artificial lake and island, wild
areas of cypress and ilex trees and various follies. The gardens
were full of precious works of art – Michelangelo's *Quattro Prigioni*
(now in the Accademia) were once here, as was Giambologna's
Oceanus (now in the Bargello). Happily, many originals are still here,
including the classical statues that line the cypress avenue known
as Viottolone.

The gardens get packed out in summer but if you want to get
away from the crowds use the entrance in Via Romana and wander
down to the southwest corner. Don't miss the amphitheatre, built
out of the quarry, as well as La Grotta Grande and the artificial

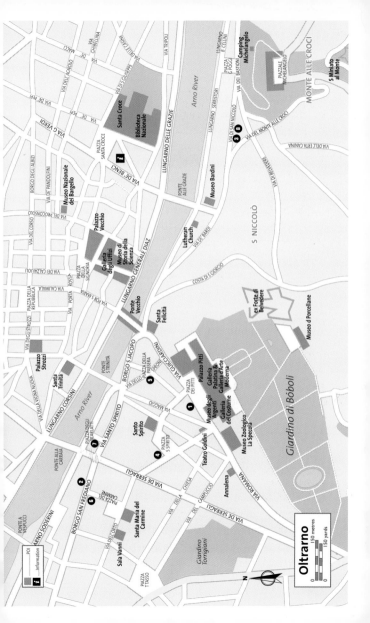

A PIAZZA WITH A VIEW

A stirring walk up from the river, Piazzale Michelangelo gives spectacular views over Florence and the surrounding area. Aim to reach the summit as dusk falls to see an amazing sunset, or even better, get up early and watch the sun rise over the city. If you don't fancy the climb, hop on Bus 12 or 13.

⬇ *Watch the sun set over the Arno from Piazzale Michelangelo*

island of L'Isolotto. ❷ Piazza dei Pitti ❶ 055 23885 ❺ 08.15–17.30 daily (Mar); 08.15–18.30 daily (Apr, May, Sept & Oct); 08.15–19.30 daily (June–Aug); 08.15–16.30 daily (Nov–Feb); closed first & last Mon of the month ❽ Bus: C3, D, 36, 37 ❶ Admission charge

Museo Bardini (Bardini Museum)

Architectural salvage is all the rage in modern cities these days, but Stefano Bardini had the good sense to do it in the 19th century when all kinds of medieval and Renaissance buildings were being demolished to make way for the Piazza della Repubblica. Palazzo

Bardini, built in 1883, contains mostly salvaged medieval and Renaissance stonework and carpentry. There are no famous exhibits but the place is full of treasures Bardini snapped up or found among the ruins and rubble. ❸ Via dei Renai 37 ❶ 055 226 4042 ❷ 11.00–17.00 Sat–Mon ❷ Bus: C3, D, 13, 23 ❶ Admission charge

Museo Zoologico La Specola (La Specola Museum)

This natural history museum, deep in the university buildings, makes a real change from frescoes and sculpture. The *Cere Anatomiche* waxworks were created as teaching aids in the 18th century – each wax model of a dissected body displays a separate set of muscles, arteries and other internal bits and pieces. If that isn't graphic enough, there is a tableau representing the horrors of the plague. ❸ Via Romana 17 ❶ 055 228 8251 ❷ 10.30–17.30 Tues–Sun ❷ Bus: 36, 37, 68 ❶ Admission charge

Palazzo Pitti

The main residence of the Medici family after their move from Palazzo Vecchio, this place expanded with time. When Florence was briefly the capital of Italy it become the home of the Italian royals, but now it is a complex of museums, the best of which is the Galleria Palatina (see pages 104–5). Also in here are the royal apartments, a sumptuous spread of 18th- and 19th-century magnificence – ornate ceilings, enormous four-poster beds and paintings of the Medici. The Parrot Room is covered in beautiful silk cloth, detailed with bird designs. Also worth a visit is the Galleria del Costume (see page 104), the carriage museum, the Museo degli Argenti (see page 105) and the Galleria d'Arte Moderna (see page 104). ❸ Piazza dei Pitti ❶ 055 238 8614

ⓦ www.firenzemusei.it ⓛ 08.15–18.50 Tues–Sun ⓝ Bus: C3, D, 36, 37
ⓘ Admission charge

San Miniato al Monte

The 13th-century façade of San Miniato al Monte is covered in green and white inlaid marble. Legend tells that a church was built here after St Miniatus was decapitated in AD 250 down by the river, then picked up his own head and climbed the hill to this spot. The nave has more inlaid marble, there are lovely old frescoes on the walls and there's an 11th-century barrel-vaulted crypt. Photographs are allowed and entrance is free. Surrounding the church are its burial grounds, the grand mausoleums stacked one above the other. ⓐ Via delle Porte Sante 34 ⓣ 055 234 2731 ⓛ 08.00–19.30 daily (summer); 08.00–12.00 & 14.30–18.00 daily (winter) ⓝ Bus: 12

Santo Spirito

Set in the disarmingly parochial Piazza Santo Spirito, this beautiful church was designed for the most part by Brunelleschi, but only completed after his death. The exterior was never finished but was planned to follow the unusual outlines of the 38 chapels surrounding the central nave. Admire the elaborate architecture of the interior and look out for Filippino Lippi's *Madonna and Child* in the Nerli Chapel. The crucifix in the sacristy is believed to be the work of Michelangelo. ⓐ Piazza Santo Spirito ⓣ 055 210 030 ⓛ 09.30–12.30 & 16.00–17.30 Mon, Tues & Thur–Sat, 16.00–17.30 Sun ⓝ Bus: D, 36, 37

Via Maggio

When the Medici family moved out to the Oltrarno, they made this side of the river into a much more desirable area and there followed a spree of *palazzo* building during the 15th and 16th centuries. The *palazzi* in this street are not open to the public but many of them now house antiques shops on the ground floors, which you can browse to admire the interiors. Bus: C3, 36, 37

CULTURE

Galleria d'Arte Moderna (Gallery of Modern Art)

This gallery of modern art is only modern in relation to the age of everything else in Florence. Visit the top floor of the Palazzo Pitti to view paintings from as early as 1784. The majority of the works here come from the art collection of the Dukes of Lorraine, who lived in the palace for a while. There are about 30 rooms of paintings but the highlight is the work of the 19th-century Italian Impressionists known as *Macchiaioli*, which means 'spot makers'. Piazza dei Pitti 055 238 8616 08.15–18.50 Tues–Sun; also open 2nd & 4th Mon of the month Bus: C3, D, 36, 37 Admission charge

Galleria del Costume (Costume Gallery)

Fashion fans should check out the Palazzo Pitti complex's Costume Gallery. Amassed over 200 years, the collection includes everything from corsets to miniskirts. Palazzina della Meridiana, Palazzo Pitti 055 238 8713 08.15–17.30 Tues–Sat (Mar); 08.15–18.30 Tues–Sat (Apr, May, Sept & Oct); 08.15–18.50 Tues–Sat (June–Aug); 08.15–16.30 Tues–Sat (Nov–Feb); also open 2nd & 4th Mon of the month & 1st, 3rd & 5th Sun of the month Bus: C3, D, 36, 37 Admission charge

Galleria Palatina

If this were Florence's only art gallery, you would still think it was worth the trip. The collection of more than 1,000 paintings is not arranged in chronological order. Instead, the works are left where the Grand Dukes placed them. There are paintings here by Botticelli, Andrea del Sarto, Tintoretto, Caravaggio, Rubens and Van Dyck. Several works by Titian are here, including his *Mary Magdalene* and *La Bella*, a portrait of an unknown woman. You can also see Raphael's *Madonna of the Chair* and his *Donna Velata*, a portrait of Raphael's mistress, who was a baker's daughter.

The rooms in which the artworks are displayed are like little galleries themselves, painted with ceiling frescoes by Pietro da Cortona. Other rooms include a suite built for Napoleon after his conquest of northern Italy in 1813. ⓐ Piazza dei Pitti ⓣ 055 238 8614 ⓛ 08.30–19.00 Tues–Sun ⓝ Bus: C3, D, 36, 37 ⓘ Admission charge

Museo degli Argenti

This place gives some indication of just how fabulously wealthy the Medici must have been. Not only did they build almost all of the city's palaces and churches, and collect a large portion of Florence's greatest works of art, they also stored up this little treasure house. Gold, silver, ivory, jewellery, Roman glassware, amber, inlaid ebony furniture and portraits of the family are all on display within the frescoed summer apartments. ⓐ Piazza dei Pitti ⓣ 055 238 8709 ⓛ 08.15–17.30 Tues–Sun (Apr–June); 08.15–19.00 Tues–Sun (July & Aug); 08.15–18.30 Tues–Sun (Sept & Oct); 08.15–16.30 Tues–Sun (Nov–Mar); also open 2nd & 4th Sun & Mon of the month ⓝ Bus: C3, D, 36, 37 ⓘ Admission charge

Santa Felicità

Possibly the oldest church in town, this building dates back almost 2,000 years and was one of the first Christian places of worship in Florence. It was dramatically remodelled by Brunelleschi in the 1420s

and Vasari in 1565, who added a passageway for the Medici to use when walking from one palace to another in order to avoid coming into contact with commoners. Inside, look out for two works by mannerist artist Pontorno, the *Annunciation* and the *Deposition*.
🅐 Piazza di Santa Felicità 🕿 055 213 018 🕒 09.00–12.00 & 15.00–18.00 Mon–Sat 🚍 Bus: C3, D

Santa Maria del Carmine

A major stop on the culture trail, this church is famous for the Capella Brancacci. The frescoes here are a perfect illustration of how chance events can have an enormous effect. They were commissioned by Felice Brancacci in the early 15th century, who paid the painter Masolino to do the work. Two years into the work Masolino went to Hungary for a while and left his young assistant to keep things going until he got back. The result was a series of frescoes on the life of St Peter by Masaccio, the assistant whose work surpassed his master's and set the standard for generations of Renaissance artists to follow. Masaccio didn't live to complete the work, which Filippino Lippi took on in 1480. It's worth getting here early to appreciate the frescoes in full.
🅐 Piazza del Carmine 🕿 055 238 2195 🕒 10.00–16.30 Mon & Wed–Sat, 13.00–16.30 Sun 🚍 Bus: D, 6, 36, 37 ℹ Admission charge

RETAIL THERAPY

The big shopping street is Via Guicciardini. Leather shoes, bags and clothing line the street. Look out for **Giotto Leather** at No 58r, **GABS** at No 130 and **Mannina** at No 16r.

Beaded Lily American jewellery designer Lily Mordà makes beautiful necklaces, earrings, bracelets and more from Venetian-style glass

beads, many of them made by her husband in the same shop.
🄰 Via Toscanella 33r, off Piazza dei Pitti 🄣 055 239 9182
🄦 www.beadedlily.com 🄛 10.00–12.30 & 14.30–19.00 Tues–Fri,
11.00–18.00 Sat 🄝 Bus: C3, D, 36, 37

Casini Accessible and affordable clothes, shoes and bags. Check out
the art on the walls. 🄰 Piazza dei Pitti 32–33r 🄦 www.casinifirenze.it
🄛 10.00–19.00 Mon–Sat, 11.00–18.00 Sun 🄝 Bus: C3, D, 36, 37

Emporium Lots of clever and amusing household objects, including
an umbrella in a box, spoons for getting olives out of the jar, crazy
clocks and paper clips shaped as dog bones. Bizarre but irresistible.
🄰 Via Guicciardini 122r 🄣 055 212 646 🄛 10.00–19.00 Mon–Sat,
11.30–17.00 Sun 🄝 Bus: C3, D, 36, 37

Giuditta Blandini Attractive, stylish clothes made using natural fibres
and dyes. 🄰 Piazza dei Pitti 6r 🄣 055 277 6276 🄦 www.stilebiologico.it
🄛 10.00–13.00 & 15.30–19.30 daily 🄝 Bus: C3, D, 36, 37

⬥ *Florence's wine shops offer great variety*

Giulio Giannini & Figlio Award-winning handmade marbled paper, books and cards. Check out the wallet-sized leather picture frames. ⓐ Piazza dei Pitti 37r ⓣ 055 212 621 ⓦ www.giuliogiannini.it ⓛ 10.00–19.00 Mon–Sat, 11.00–18.30 Sun ⓝ Bus: C3, D, 36, 37

Madova Tiny shop selling gloves made on the site since 1919. Choose your favourite model, colour and lining. ⓐ Via Guicciardini 1r ⓣ 055 239 6526 ⓦ www.madova.com ⓛ 09.30–19.00 Mon–Sat ⓝ Bus: C3, D, 36, 37

TAKING A BREAK

Caffè Pitti £–££ ❶ Good set lunch or *panini* options at this café-bar in a relatively quiet street. Open until late with a good dinner menu and jazz at weekends. ⓐ Piazza dei Pitti 9 ⓣ 055 239 9863 ⓦ www.caffepitti.it ⓛ 10.00–24.00 daily ⓝ Bus: C3, D, 36, 37

La Cité £–££ ❷ A labyrinth of book-lined rooms and a café where you can order coffee, a glass of wine or light snacks. There is a rotating exhibition of contemporary art. Pick up one of their programmes for a list of other events, including readings, concerts and exhibitions. ⓐ Borgo San Frediano 20r ⓣ 055 210 387 ⓦ www.lacitelibreria.info ⓛ Mon–Sat ⓝ Bus: D, 36, 37, 68

Il Rifrullo £–££ ❸ A favourite with the locals, friendly Il Rifrullo is good for anything from breakfast-time cappuccinos to light lunches and evening *aperitivi*, with snacks accompanied by music into the late hours. Sunday brunch is a crowd-pleaser. There's an open fire in the back for chilly days and a lovely terrace for summer evenings. ⓐ Via di San Niccolò 55r ⓣ 055 234 2621 ⓛ 08.00–02.00 daily; closed two weeks in Aug ⓝ Bus: D, 23

AFTER DARK

RESTAURANTS

Osteria Santo Spirito £–££ ❹ One of the best eateries in Piazza Santo Spirito, serving Tuscan food with a twist. ❸ Piazza Santo Spirito 16r ❶ 055 238 2383 ❿ www.osteriasantospirito.it ❶ 12.00–24.00 daily ❿ Bus: D, 36, 37

Trattoria 4 Leoni ££ ❺ This place comes into its own in the summer when the tables out in the square fill up with a lively young crowd. Tuscan cuisine. ❸ Piazza della Passera ❶ 055 218 562 ❶ 12.00–24.00 daily ❿ Bus: C3, D

Trattoria del Carmine ££ ❻ A great little neighbourhood *trattoria* with a tiny terrace where locals well outweigh the tourists. Carmine serves up delicious seasonal specialities such as porcini mushrooms, *ribollita* and *bistecca alla Fiorentina*. ❸ Piazza del Carmine 18r ❶ 055 218 601 ❶ 12.00–14.30 & 19.30–22.30 Mon–Sat; closed three weeks in Aug ❿ Bus: D, 6, 36, 37

Il Santo Bevitore ££–£££ ❼ This wine bar with a good food menu looks like a monastery refectory. Popular for an inexpensive lunch of salads, soup, pasta and some interesting main courses, it is also a nice quiet drinking spot in the evening. ❸ Via Santo Spirito 64–66r ❶ 055 211 264 ❿ www.ilsantobevitore.com ❶ 12.30–14.30 & 19.30–23.30 Mon–Sat, 19.30–23.30 Sun ❿ Bus: C3, D, 36, 37

Filipepe £££ ❽ The chefs at this shabby-chic restaurant come from the south, so the food is full of punchy, sunny flavours, with fish playing a prominent part. Try the pasta with sardines, sultanas and pine nuts. Desserts are delicious. ❸ Via di San Niccolò 39r ❶ 055 200 1397 ❿ www.filipepe.com ❺ 19.30–01.00 daily; closed two weeks in Aug ❻ Bus: D, 23

BARS & CLUBS

Dolce Vita Trendy bar with pink vinyl cushions and gold furnishings. Pop in for an *aperitivo* around 19.00 and stay for cocktails, music and mood. ❸ Piazza del Carmine ❶ 055 284 595 ❿ www.dolcevitaflorence.com ❺ 08.00–02.00 daily ❻ Bus: D, 36, 37, 68

Fuori Porta This wood-panelled wine bar is situated just outside the city gates and has a lovely terrace. There is a great choice of wines plus a menu of hot and cold snacks and more substantial dishes. ❸ Via del Monte alle Croci 10r ❶ 055 234 2483 ❿ www.fuoriporta.it ❺ 12.30–15.30 & 19.00–00.30 Mon–Sat; closed two weeks in Aug ❻ Bus: D, 13, 23

James Joyce Lively atmosphere in this trendy bar with a huge, enclosed garden. Happy hour 19.30–21.30. ❸ Lungarno Benvenuto Cellini 1r ❶ 055 658 0856 ❺ 18.00–02.00 Tues–Thur, 18.00–03.00 Fri–Sun ❻ Bus: D, 13, 23, 71

Le Volpi e L'Uva This popular little wine bar serves unusual wines by the glass and by the bottle from all over Italy. Delicious snacks include Italian and French cheeses, various types of *prosciutto* (ham) and salami and divine toasted *crostini* topped with melted cheese. ❸ Piazza de' Rossi 1r ❶ 055 239 8132 ❿ www.levolpieluva.com ❺ 11.00–21.00 Mon–Sat ❻ Bus: C3, D

---

❿ *Unmissable: the Leaning Tower of Pisa*

OUT OF TOWN
trips

Pisa

With the advent of budget airlines, Pisa is fast becoming a major hub in the Tuscan tourist industry. It last enjoyed this level of popularity in the 13th century, before the Arno River began to silt up and disconnected the city from its lucrative maritime trade. In the intervening centuries Pisa has quietly slumbered away, its medieval buildings intact and its tower leaning a little more each year until underpinning work began in 1989.

Academic institutions make the city a very young place with a lively nightlife; other attractions include the Campo dei Miracoli, some excellent shopping opportunities and plenty of good cafés.

The **tourist office** (ⓐ Piazza Arcivescovado 8 ❶ 334 641 9408 Ⓦ www.pisaturismo.it ❶ 09.30–19.30 daily) is on the edge of Piazza del Duomo, next door to the ticket office for the Campo dei Miracoli. There is another tourist office at the airport (❶ 050 502 518).

GETTING THERE

Pisa is located approximately 80 km (50 miles) west of Florence. You can take the Terravision bus (Ⓦ www.terravision.eu) from Piazza della Stazione in Florence. Departure times are listed in front of the departure point (ⓐ Via Alamanni), where you can buy tickets. Reserve a seat at weekends.

There is also a regular train service from Florence to Pisa. Train travel is inexpensive (around six euros for a single ticket) and is the best way to see the surrounding countryside. See Ⓦ http://trenitalia.it

If you're driving from Florence to Pisa, take the A11 to Pisa Nord and then head south for about 6 km (4 miles) on the SS1 Aurelia, following the signs for 'Centro'.

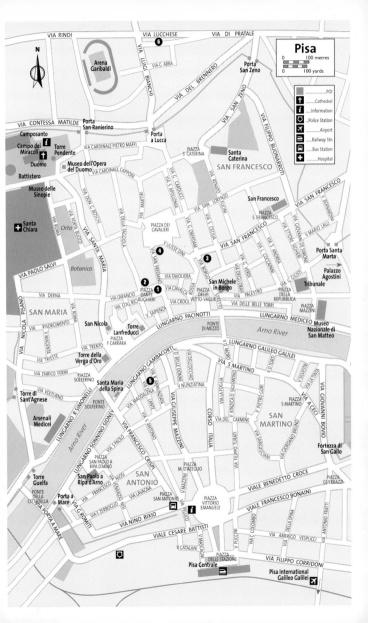

● *The immense Baptistery in the Campo dei Miracoli*

There are only a few buses which circle around within the city, leaving from the train station and the airport. Pisa is tiny and in general is best navigated on foot.

SIGHTS & ATTRACTIONS

Battistero (Baptistery)

Older than the church buildings at the heart of Florence, this Baptistery dates back to Pisa's time as the leading mercantile light during the 12th century, although the domed roof is a later 14th-century addition. The 1260 pulpit was designed by Nicola Pisano and carved with scenes from the life of Christ. ❸ Campo dei Miracoli ❶ 050 387 2211 ❤ www.opapisa.it ❶ 09.00–18.00 daily (Mar); 08.00–20.00 daily (Apr–Sept); 09.00–19.00 daily (Oct); 10.00–17.00 daily (Nov–Feb) ❶ Admission charge

Campo dei Miracoli (Field of Miracles)

The Field of Miracles is one of the most photographed places in the world. The lawns containing the leaning tower, the Duomo and the Baptistery make a good sight in themselves. Come here on a busy day, take a photo of yourself pretending to hold up the tower, or pick up a cheap souvenir from the stalls selling all manner of leaning tower memorabilia, including tea towels, T-shirts, plastic models, chocolate and umbrellas.

Camposanto

The cemetery where important Pisans were buried is lined by a cloistered wall which used to display a series of 14th-century frescoes by Benozzo Gozzoli. An Allied plane bombed them in 1944 and the few which survived depict, appropriately enough, visions of

hell and death. ⏰ 09.00–18.00 daily (Mar); 08.00–20.00 daily
(Apr–Sept); 09.00–19.00 daily (Oct); 10.00–17.00 daily (Nov–Feb)
❶ Admission charge

Duomo (Cathedral)

Pisa's cathedral, begun in 1063, beats the one in Florence in age
if not in size. The impressive façade is 12th century and inlaid with
glass, majolica and sandstone knots, flowers and animals. Lower
down is plain white marble. High up in the west façade is the tomb
of Buscheto, the architect of the building.

Much of the cathedral's interior was damaged by a fire in
1595. Paintings and the pulpit, lost in the fire, were replaced thanks
to Medici money from Florence. At the eastern side is the Portale
San Ranieri, with bronze doors by Bonnano Pisano dating back to
1180. Here, as in the rest of the exterior, there are Arab influences
in the bronze designs and in the patterns in the inlaid façade.
🄰 Campo dei Miracoli ☎ 050 560 547 🔵 www.opapisa.it
⏰ 10.00–18.00 daily (Mar); 10.00–20.00 daily (Apr–Sept); 10.00–
19.00 daily (Oct); 10.00–12.45 & 14.00–17.00 daily (Nov–Feb)
❶ Admission charge

Orto Botanico (Botanic Garden)

A pleasant spot for a picnic, this is the oldest botanic garden
in Europe. 🄰 Via Luca Ghini 5, off Via Santa Maria ☎ 050 551 345
⏰ 08.30–17.00 Mon–Fri, 08.00–13.00 Sat

Piazza dei Cavalieri (Square of the Knights)

This is the heart of Pisa's student quarter, a wide open square
surrounded by *palazzi*. On the north side is the Palazzo dei Cavalieri,
designed by Vasari as the headquarters of the Cavalieri de San

A FATHER'S REVENGE

Opposite the Palazzo dei Cavalieri is the Palazzo dell'Orologico, and inside that is the medieval jail where the mayor Count Ugolino was imprisoned in 1288 for treachery. He was walled up along with his sons and grandsons and, the story goes, ate them in order to stay alive. In Dante's *Inferno* Count Ugolino is condemned to hell where he feeds forever on the head of Archbishop Ruggieri, the man who denounced him.

Stefano, an order of knights created by Cosimo I. It is currently a university building.

Before this 16th-century building was constructed, the site was home to the medieval town hall. All but the council chamber, which still survives as a lecture theatre, was demolished when the city came under Medici rule.

The man on the horse in the square is Cosimo himself. Beside it is the *Chiesa dei Cavalieri* or 'Knight's Church', the walls of which are hung with the battle standards of the knights.

Torre Pendente (Leaning Tower)

Go against the grain and ignore the fact that the tower is leaning in order to appreciate it as a beautiful piece of architecture. It is eight storeys high and hollow at its core. Inside, a spiral staircase works its way up to the belfry, where there are seven bells. Six of the storeys contain colonnaded galleries reached by doors in the staircase. To climb the tower you must book either online or at the booking office in person in advance, at least 15 days before you plan to visit. The climb is pricey but worth it. ⓐ Campo dei Miracoli

ⓦ www.opapisa.it ⓛ 09.30–17.30 daily (Feb & Nov); 09.00–17.30 daily (Mar); 08.30–20.00 daily (Apr–Sept); 09.00–19.00 daily (Oct); 10.00–16.30 daily (Dec & Jan) ⓘ Admission charge

San Nicola

This tiny 11th-century church dedicated to Pisa's patron saint contains a painting showing Pisa during the plague. Its *campanile* also leans. ⓐ Via Santa Maria 2 ⓣ 050 24677 ⓛ 08.30–12.00 & 17.00–19.00 daily

---

A LUCRATIVE ERROR

Pisa's most visited tourist attraction, its leaning tower, was a bit of a disaster from the very start. Begun in 1173, it took nearly 200 years to build and was already leaning by 1274 when the fourth storey was added. By 1350, when the tower was finally finished, it was 1.4 m (5 ft) off-kilter and it continued to slide a little more each year for six centuries. By 1993 it was 5.4 m (18 ft) askew. The reason? The tower was built on sand.

Work began in 1989 to correct the lean, although for a time things got slightly worse. Underpinning has corrected the lean by about 40 cm (16 in) and the tower is considered safe once more, although only 30 people are allowed in at a time. The tower is attractive, but in itself would hardly be interesting – it is because of, rather than in spite of, its faults that it draws so many tourists to the city. It's not recommended that architects should follow the same path, but in this case building on sand proved to be a lucrative error indeed.

◢ Pisa's Palazzo dei Cavalieri dominates the Square of the Knights

San Paolo a Ripa d'Arno

This 12th-century church, built in the same style as the Duomo, has an impressive façade. Inside is a chapel dedicated to St Agatha which is built, unusually, entirely of brick, including its cone-shaped roof. ⓐ Piazza San Paolo a Ripa d'Arno ① 050 41515 ① By arrangement only

Santa Maria della Spina (St Mary of the Thorn)

This tiny white Gothic church isn't named after the many spiny rills and flutes of its exterior, but after one of the thorns from the crown on Christ's head which was allegedly kept here for a time. ⓐ Lungarno Gambacorti ① 10.00–14.00 Tues–Sun, usually open longer in summer

CULTURE

Museo dell'Opera del Duomo

This building was once the chapter house of the cathedral and now holds monuments from the piazza, Duomo and Baptistery. You can see the exquisite inlay work close up and there are good displays explaining the exhibits. There are also collections of Roman and Etruscan remains and good views of the tower from the cloister. ⓐ Piazza dell'Arcivescovado 8 ① 050 835 011 ① 09.00–17.30 daily (Mar); 08.30–20.00 daily (Apr–Sept); 09.00–19.00 daily (Oct); 10.00–17.00 daily (Nov–Feb) ① Admission charge

Museo delle Sinopie

When World War II was over and people began to pick up the pieces in the Camposanto they discovered that, although the frescoes had disintegrated, the outlines that the artists had drawn underneath in the original layer of plaster were intact. These have been reconstructed and brought together in this museum and give a fascinating insight into the technicalities of the work of the artists. ❷ Piazza del Duomo ❶ 09.00–17.30 daily (Mar); 08.30–20.00 daily (Apr–Sept); 09.00–19.00 daily (Oct); 10.00–17.00 daily (Nov–Feb) ❶ Admission charge

Museo Nazionale di San Matteo

Once the medieval convent of San Matteo, this attractive Gothic building now houses the slightly disorganised Pisan art collection. While the medieval works are well worth seeing, particularly Nino Pisano's *Madonna del Latte*, the museum's real gems are the Renaissance paintings. There are works here by Masaccio, Donatello, Fra Angelico and Ghirlandaio. ❷ Piazza San Matteo in Soarta ❶ 050 541 865 ❶ 08.30–19.00 Mon–Sat, 08.30–13.00 Sun ❶ Admission charge

RETAIL THERAPY

The two main shopping streets in town are Borgo Stretto and Corso Italia, and although neither of them come up to the luxury shopping standards of Siena or Florence, there are a few good places to check out.

Corso Italia is the more respectable shopping street. Its small shops, still mostly family-run businesses, now compete for space with the usual suspects such as H&M, Intimissimi and Benetton. At the end of the street is an arcaded market selling second-hand books. Look out for **Di Banchi** at No 3, selling fashionable clothes and shoes, while next door is a very traditional shoe shop.

Borgo Stretto is more avant-garde, lined with interesting boutiques as well as a small tourist market. Adjoining the street in Piazza delle Vettovaglie is a daily fruit and vegetable market, where *cavolo nero* (kale) and globe artichokes are on sale alongside more ordinary produce.

Around the square you'll find some interesting shops selling jewellery and other potential gifts. **Delicatessen Cesqui** at No 38 (☎ 050 580 269 ● 07.00–13.30 & 16.00–20.00 daily) is a great place to pick up supplies for a picnic. Right next door to it is an excellent bakery.

TAKING A BREAK

Caffeteria Dantesca £ ❶ The best of several café-bars in this quiet, green square, this place serves pizzas, pasta dishes and filled rolls as well as ice cream and cakes. ● Piazza Dante Alighieri ☎ 050 46280 ● 08.30–24.00 daily

Café Pasticceria Macchi £ ❷ Set in the quiet Piazza Dante Alighieri, this café-bar serves lots of tasty snacks and more substantial dishes, along with the usual wine and espresso at the bar. Tables outside. ● Via Tanucci 7, off Piazza Dante Alighieri ☎ 050 56100 ● 06.30–19.00 daily

Salza £–££ ❸ Pretty tables under the loggia of the building, which offer good cakes and sweets as well as a full restaurant menu. ● Via Borgo Stretto 46 ☎ 050 580 144 ● 07.45–20.30 daily

🔺 *Enjoy an alfresco meal in one of the city's many pavement cafés*

AFTER DARK

RESTAURANTS

Osteria dei Cavalieri ££ ❹ Popular with students and staff from the university, this inexpensive place is set in a medieval tower house. Lunch specials are particularly good value and the evening menu offers some excellent traditional Tuscan food. ❸ Via San Frediano 16 ❶ 050 580 858 ❶ 12.30–14.00 & 19.30–22.00 Mon–Fri, 19.30–22.00 Sat

Le Repubbliche Marinare ££–£££ ❺ On a quiet side street just east of Santa Maria della Spina, this restaurant serves creative fish and seafood dishes as well as pizza. ❸ Vicolo Ricciardi 8, off Lungarno Gambacorti ❶ 050 20506 ❼ www.repubblichemarinare.eu ❶ 20.00–23.00 Tues–Sun (July & Aug); 12.30–14.30 & 20.00–23.00 Tues–Sun (Sept–June)

Aphrodite £££ ❻ A little way out of the centre of town, this place is worth seeking out for its modern design and creative cooking. In summer, eat out in the cool of the garden. ❸ Via Lucchese 33a ❶ 050 830 248 ❼ www.ristoranteaphrodite.it ❶ 13.00–15.30 & 20.00–24.00 Mon–Fri, 20.00–24.00 Sat

BARS & CLUBS

Borderline Occasional live music in this laid-back place, focusing on blues and country. ❸ Via Vernaccini 7 ❶ 050 58077 ❼ www.borderlineclub.it ❶ 21.00–02.00 Mon–Sat ❶ Admission charge for live music

Dottorjazz Jazz club with lots of atmosphere close to the railway station. ❸ Via Amerigo Vespucci 10 ❶ 339 861 9298 ❶ 21.00–02.00 Tues–Sat (Oct–May) ❶ Admission charge

ACCOMMODATION

HOTELS

Hotel Roseto £ One of the best bargains in Pisa, this central two-star hotel has airy rooms, a pretty garden and a roof terrace with lovely views. 🅐 Via Mascagani 24 🅣 050 42596 🅦 www.hotelroseto.it 🅝 Bus: 2, 4, 5, 6, 13, 14, 21, 22, Lam Verde, Lam Rosso, Lam Blu

Hotel Novecento ££ Ten rooms beautifully decorated with designer pieces including Philippe Starck and Dolce & Gabbana, just steps from the Piazza dei Miracoli. 🅐 Via Roma 37 🅣 050 500 323 🅕 050 220 9163 🅦 www.hotelnovecento.pisa.it 🅝 Bus: 4, 21, Lam Rosso

Hotel Repubblica Marinara ££ All modern conveniences in this purpose-built small hotel, about 1 km (½ mile) from the town centre. Internet access, great breakfast and a courtesy bus to anywhere in town. 🅐 Via Matteucci 81 🅣 050 387 0100 🅦 www.hotelrepubblica marinara.it 🅝 Bus: Lam Blu

Royal Victoria ££ A central hotel with a roof terrace and views over the river, catering to tourists for over 100 years. Lots of charm. 🅐 Lungarno Pacinotti 12 🅣 050 940 111 🅦 www.royalvictoria.it 🅝 Bus: 2, 4, 14, Lam Verde, Lam Rosso

B&Bs

Albergo Galileo £ Basic B&B, centrally located, with original frescoes on the walls. Only nine rooms. 🅐 Via Santa Maria 12 🅣 050 40621 🅦 www.pisaonline.it/hotelgalileo 🅝 Bus: E

Siena

A perfect size for a day trip, Siena has a sense of calm and openness that Florence often lacks. Coaches are rarely in evidence as you wander through the ancient twisting streets as almost all of the city centre is pedestrianised; you may even find yourself alone in one of the city squares during the afternoon closing period.

The heart of the city is the stunning Piazza del Campo, bristling with cafés that offer prime people-watching. A long street heads south from the bus terminus, lined with shops. To the west, the winding streets lead to the Duomo while to the south is the Botanic Garden, free of charge and the perfect spot for a picnic lunch. North and west of the bus terminus is the Piazza San Domenico and its huge monastery.

Tourist office ⓐ Piazza del Campo 56 ⓣ 057 728 0551 ⓦ www.terresiena.it

GETTING THERE

Located 70 km (44 miles) south of Florence, Siena is best accessed by bus. SITA buses (ⓣ 800 373 760 ⓦ www.sitabus.it) depart every 30 minutes from the terminal in Via Santa Caterina da Siena. Journey time is an hour and a quarter. Take the *Corse Rapide* (Express) bus or you will visit several towns en route.

Trains also make the journey from Santa Maria Novella station, but usually involve changing trains at Empoli and a journey time of two hours. ⓦ http://trenitalia.it

If you're driving from Florence to Siena, head south on the Firenze–Siena superstrada, or for a more scenic route, take the Chiantigiana 222 to Siena's city centre.

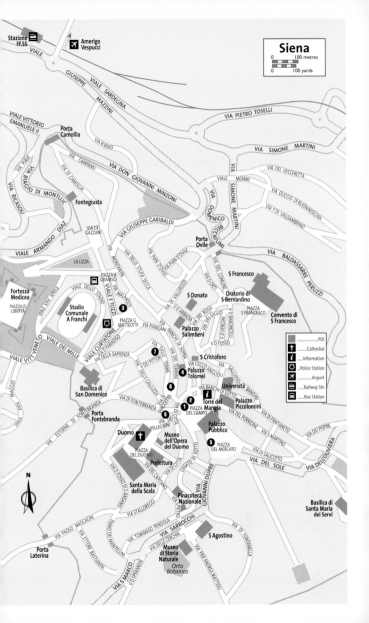

◆ *The unmistakable striped interior of the Duomo*

SIGHTS & ATTRACTIONS

Basilica di San Domenico

This Dominican monastery is where St Catherine had her visions
and bore stigmata. Her head is encased in a marble tabernacle on
the altar. Frescoes around the chapel are by Sodoma and show
St Catherine in a state of ecstasy. There is a contemporary painting
of her in the church by Giovanni di Stefano. The building is mostly
the result of 20th-century restoration work. ⓐ Piazza San Domenico
ⓘ 0577 28901 ⓒ 07.00–18.30 daily (Mar–Oct); 09.00–18.00 daily
(Nov–Feb)

Duomo (Cathedral)

The open plan for this 12th-century church showed it was to be
the biggest in Christendom. Work was well under way in the
14th century when the plague hit the city. What remains is perhaps
just as fascinating as what might have been – the unfinished nave
stands, looking like a demolition site to the southwest of the church.

The earlier Gothic building is covered by a black and white
marble façade, designed in part by Giovanni Pisano. Inside, the inlaid
marble floors are also out of sight for most of the year and opened
only in autumn.

Some big names worked on the inside of this church, including
Arnolfo di Cambio, who also worked on Florence's Duomo. Nicolas
Pisano and son built the pulpit and Michelangelo cast the statues
of the saints on the Piccolomini altar. The frescoes in the Libreria
Piccolomini, a library built within the Duomo in 1495 to house the
books of Pope Pius II, are by Pinturicchio and his young assistant
Raphael. Beside the church is the unfinished Baptistery with its
central font by Ghiberti, Donatello and Jacopo della Quercia.

❸ Piazza del Duomo ❶ 057 747 321 ❷ 10.30–19.30 Mon–Sat,
13.30–17.30 Sun (Mar–May); 10.30–20.00 Mon–Sat, 13.30–18.30 Sun
(June–Aug); 10.30–19.30 daily (Sept & Oct); 10.30–18.30 Mon–Sat,
13.30–17.30 Sun (Nov–Feb) ❶ Admission charge

Fortezza Medicea (Medici Fortress) & Enoteca Italiana (National Wine Museum)

The Fortezza Medicea was constructed in 1562 under the orders of
Charles V of Spain, demolished when Siena became independent of
Spanish rule and then built again on the orders of Cosimo de Medici
after an 18-month siege by the Florentines. The square inside the
fortress is ironically called Piazza della Libertà (Freedom Square).
The courtyard has recently been turned into a public park and is
a nice rural spot for an evening stroll with views over the city.

THE SIENESE PALIO

If you are in Tuscany on 2 July or 16 August, you, along with
thousands of others, will probably be at Italy's most famous
horse-racing festival in Siena's Piazza del Campo. The enormous
square fills up to breaking point and vast sums change hands
with those people lucky enough to own a window with a view
of the piazza. The 17 city districts, or *contrade*, choose their horse
and rider by drawing lots and several preliminary races take
place to choose the entries. The real race starts at about 19.00
and the three laps of the campo take about 90 seconds. Jockeys
ride bareback and rivalry is real and fierce; horses occasionally
break legs and sadly have to be put down, while the winners
brag about their victory for the whole of the following year.

Inside the fortress is the Enoteca Italiana, Italy's national wine museum, where you can sample an extensive range of Tuscan and Italian wines along with cold plates of typical regional foods.
ⓘ 0577 288 843 ⓦ www.enoteca-italiana.it ⓛ 10.00–01.00 Mon–Sat

Orto Botanico (Botanic Garden)
Two hectares (5 acres) of garden, entirely free, in which to wander around and picnic. ⓐ Via Pier Andrea Mattioli 4 ⓘ 057 723 2874
ⓛ 08.00–12.30 & 14.30–17.30 Mon–Fri, 08.00–12.00 Sat

Palazzo Pubblico (Town Hall)
This 14th-century building still functions as the city hall but several rooms are open to the public. In the Sala del Mappa Mundo (Map of

● The thrilling action of the Palio

the World Room) you will find the *Maestà* of Simone Martini along with his portrait of a mercenary soldier, Guidoriccio da Fogliano.

In the adjacent chapel are 15th-century frescoes by Taddeo di Bartolo and choir stalls with intricately carved and inlaid panels showing scenes from the Bible. The best works are in the Sala de Pace (Peace Room), including Lorenzetti's *Allegory of Good and Bad Government*. ⓐ Piazza del Campo 🕿 057 729 2263 🕒 10.00–19.00 daily (summer); 10.00–18.00 daily (winter) ❶ Admission charge

Piazza del Campo & Torre del Mangia

This 14th-century brick bell tower – built to be the highest in Italy – is 102 m (335 ft) high and contains 503 steps which the bell ringers had to climb several times a day. Only 15 people at a time can climb the tower, so book early at the Museo Civico ticket office if you want to see the views over the Piazza del Campo.

The shell-shaped Piazza del Campo was originally a Roman forum, lying in the base of the surrounding hills and divided into nine segments for the medieval city's nine council members. The fountain at the northern end dates back to 1408, its marble figures replaced with replicas in the 19th century.

Tower ⓐ Piazza del Campo 🕒 10.00–19.00 daily (Mar–mid-Oct); 10.00–16.00 daily (mid-Oct–Feb) ❶ Admission charge

CULTURE

Museo dell'Opera del Duomo

Built into the side aisle of the unfinished nave, this museum houses the Pisano sculptures from the façade of the building as well as Duccio di Buoninsegna's *Pala della Maestà* (1308), which was originally the high altar of the Duomo. One side features the Madonna with saints,

⬥ *Siena's enormous Piazza del Campo*

while the other has scenes from the life of Christ. From the loggia of the museum there are views over the city. ⓐ Piazza del Duomo 8 ⓣ 057 728 3048 ⓛ 09.30–19.00 daily (Mar–May, Sept & Oct); 09.30–20.00 daily (June–Aug); 10.00–17.00 daily (Nov–Feb) ⓘ Admission charge

Pinacoteca Nazionale (National Gallery)

The artists of Siena followed a different path to the naturalistic style of Botticelli and this can be seen in this museum and gallery set in the 14th-century Palazzo Buonsignori. There are over 1,500 works of art here and the Siena school is well represented with their characteristic gilded backgrounds, or *fondi d'oro*. Highlights are Lorenzetti's *Two Views*, painted in the 14th century and showing a rare use of landscape painting, and Pietro Domenico's *Adoration of the Shepherds* (1510) showing the typical gilded background style. ⓐ Via San Pietro 29 ⓣ 057 728 1161 ⓛ 08.15–19.15 Tues–Sat, 09.00–13.00 Sun & Mon ⓘ Admission charge

Santa Maria della Scala

This erstwhile hospital for pilgrims, still in use up to the 1980s, is now a museum with its original frescoes of hospital life still on the walls. Mostly home to temporary exhibitions, there is also a small archaeological museum. ⓐ Piazza del Duomo 2 ⓣ 057 722 4811 ⓦ www.santamariadellascala.com ⓛ 10.30–18.30 daily (summer); 10.30–16.30 daily (winter) ⓘ Admission charge

RETAIL THERAPY

The main streets Banchi di Sopra and Via di Città are home to the best of the city's shops. Lots of familiar names are here, especially along Banchi di Sopra, including **Benetton**, **Footlocker** and **Max Mara**. Some local clothes shops include **Extyn**, **Bloom** and the department store **UPIM**, which is inexpensive and worth a browse. **Mori** in Banchi di Sopra has designer shoes, bags and jackets in leather and **Yamamay** at No 62 has fashionable underwear. On Wednesday mornings the market along Piazza La Lizza is fun to browse, while an antiques market is held on some Sundays in the Piazza del Mercato.

Drago Rosso Artefacts from around the world, including jumpers from Ecuador, tapestries from India, teapots, ethnic jewellery and interesting clothes. ❷ Via dei Pellegrini 13 ❶ 057 728 5102 ❸ 10.00–20.00 daily

La Fabbrica delle Candele Siena Everything you can think of made of wax, including flowers, dolphins and Buddhas. Check out the lovely candles which are handmade and painted in the shop. ❷ Via dei Pellegrini ❶ 057 723 6417 ❿ www.lafabbricadellecandele.com ❸ 09.30–19.30 Mon–Wed, Fri & Sat, 10.00–19.30 Sun

La Fontana della Frutta Fresh fruit, gorgeous cakes, nuts, cheeses, olive oil, salamis, bread and filled rolls. ❷ Via delle Terme 65–67 ❶ 057 740 422 ❸ 08.00–20.00 Mon–Sat

Morbidi More than just a delicatessen shop, this has stacks of pickled and bottled goodies, cooked meats, vegetables swimming in oil, wine and lots more for a picnic lunch. ❷ Via Banchi di Sopra 75 ❶ 057 728 0268 ❸ 09.00–20.00 Mon–Sat

Swarovski Delectable glass goods including delicate jewellery, ornaments and *objets d'art* with prices to match. ❷ Via di Città 11 ❶ 057 744 572 ❸ 09.30–17.30 Mon–Fri

TAKING A BREAK

La Costarella £ ❶ Ice cream parlour with the usual array of flavours, cakes and coffee. ⓐ Via di Città 33 ⓣ 057 728 8076 ⓛ 08.30–24.00 Fri–Wed (summer); 08.30–21.00 Fri–Wed (winter)

Fiorella £ ❷ Tiny café with only one or two seats. ⓐ Via di Città 13 ⓣ 057 727 1255 ⓛ 07.00–19.00 daily

Nannini £ ❸ Good all-round cake, coffee and snack shop, close to the bus terminus. More substantial dishes of pasta and ciabatta are available at lunchtime. ⓐ Piazza G Matteotti ⓣ 057 728 3282 ⓛ 07.00–20.00 Mon–Sat, 07.30–20.00 Sun

Nannini £ ❹ A second branch of the popular Nannini chain, offering cakes and rolls, good cappuccino and a huge buffet lunch from 12.00. Stand at the bar for an inexpensive coffee and cake or sit down for the waitress service, which costs slightly more. ⓐ Via Banchi di Sopra 24 ⓣ 057 723 6009 ⓛ 07.30–21.00 daily

La Finestra ££ ❺ Busy, bright, well-kept restaurant with tables outside in the market square. Usual menu of salads, pasta (including *pici*, the traditional pasta of Siena), some interesting main courses and *carpaccio* (thinly sliced raw meat). Aimed largely at the local market with no English-language menu. ⓐ Piazza del Mercato 14 ⓣ 057 722 3502 ⓛ 12.00–15.00 & 19.00–22.00 Mon–Sat

AFTER DARK

Nightlife here is a fairly quiet affair – families eat late and make an evening of it. There are several bars in town aimed at the tourist market, including a couple with live music at weekends. Look for **Maudit** (ⓐ Vicolo della Fortuna 21, off Via di Salicotto ⓣ 057 746 818 ⓛ 20.00–late daily) or the **Tea Room** (ⓐ Porta Giustizia 11, bottom of the steps in Via dei Malcontenti ⓣ 057 722 2753 ⓛ Until 03.00 daily).

RESTAURANTS

Enoteca I Terzi ££ ⓺ A wine bar in a red-brick, candlelit room. Come for lunch or dinner and stay for the wine. Small menu up on a blackboard changes each day. ⓐ Via dei Termini 7 ⓣ 057 744 329 ⓦ www.enotecaiterzi.it ⓛ 12.30–14.30 & 19.30–22.30 Mon–Sat

Compagnia dei Vinattieri ££–£££ ⓻ Stylish, tastefully decorated basement dining room with high stone arches and a welcoming atmosphere. Try the pasta with wild boar, ravioli with pigeon or rabbit with olives – all traditional Tuscan fare. ⓐ Via delle Terme 79 ⓣ 057 723 6568 ⓦ www.vinattieri.net ⓛ 12.30–14.30 & 19.30–22.00 daily

Da Mugolone £££ ⓼ Classy, quiet and spacious yet affordable. Classic Sienese dishes such as fried calf brain, pheasant cooked in foil and fried rabbit. Less adventurous visitors could go for the beef with garlic and rosemary. Exciting desserts. ⓐ Via dei Pellegrini 8 ⓣ 057 728 3235 ⓛ 12.30–15.00 & 19.30–22.00 Mon–Wed, Fri & Sat, 12.30–15.00 Sun

ACCOMMODATION

HOTELS & APARTMENTS

Antica Torre ££ Possibly the best-value place in town, this small hotel is in a renovated 16th-century tower with rooftop views. Lots of atmosphere and close to all the sights. Book well in advance. ⓐ Via di Fiera Vecchia 7, off Via dell'Oliviera ⓣ 057 722 2255 ⓦ www.anticatorresiena.it ⓔ anticatorre@email.it

Borgo Grondaie ££–£££ Two km (1¼ miles) from Siena city centre but close to the train station, this group of converted farmhouses is an oasis of tranquillity. Perfect for families or groups of friends. No public transport. ⓐ Strada delle Grondaie 15 ⓣ 057 733 2539 ⓕ 0577 335 761 ⓦ www.borgogrondaie.com

CAMPSITES

Colleverde £ Campsite 3 km (2 miles) outside the city with a bar, café, pool and shop. No public transport. ⓐ Strada Scacciapensieri 47 ⓣ 057 733 2545 ⓦ www.sienacamping.com ⓛ Apr–Oct

ⓓ *Palazzo Vecchio, Florence*

PRACTICAL
information

Directory

GETTING THERE

By air

Meridiana (ⓦ www.meridiana.it) flies direct between London
Gatwick and Florence's Amerigo Vespucci airport twice daily.
There are regular direct flights from Paris with Air France
(ⓦ www.airfrance.com), from Milan and Rome with Alitalia
(ⓦ www.alitalia.com) or from Munich or Frankfurt with Lufthansa
(ⓦ www.lufthansa.com).

🔺 *The brand-new Tramvia tram system is a handy way of getting around*

Around 20 airlines offer direct flights to Pisa's Galileo Galilei airport from almost 50 cities worldwide, though many operate only in the summer. Most long-haul flights are booked through Rome or Milan.

British Airways flies from London Gatwick and Heathrow.
☎ 0844 493 0787 Ⓦ www.britishairways.com

Delta now operates regular flights from New York to Pisa.
Ⓦ www.delta.com

easyJet flies to Pisa from London Gatwick, Luton and Bristol.
Ⓦ www.easyjet.com

Jet2 flies from Belfast, Leeds Bradford, Manchester and Newcastle.
☎ 0871 226 1737 Ⓦ www.jet2.com

Ryanair flies to Pisa from Bournemouth, Doncaster, Dublin, East Midlands, Glasgow, Liverpool and London Stansted.
Ⓦ www.ryanair.com

Thomson Fly flies from Bournemouth, Coventry, Doncaster, London Gatwick and Manchester. ☎ 0871 231 4787 Ⓦ www.thomsonfly.com

Many people are aware that air travel emits CO_2, which contributes to climate change. You may be interested in the possibility of lessening the environmental impact of your flight through the charity **Climate Care** (Ⓦ www.jpmorganclimatecare.com), which offsets your CO_2 by funding environmental projects around the world.

By car

It will take approximately two days to cover the 1,500 km (930 miles) from London to Florence. From Calais head south in the direction of Basel, passing Milan and then getting on the A1 to Florence.

By coach

Buses connect Florence with many European cities. Coach fares are generally lower than the equivalent journey by train although the journey does take longer. For specific information regarding schedules and prices, check:

Eurolines ☎ 0870 514 3219 Ⓦ www.eurolines.com

National Express ☎ 0870 580 8080 Ⓦ www.nationalexpress.com

By rail

To take the train from the UK to Florence, first take the Eurostar to Paris. There is an overnight train from Paris to Florence which departs at about 18.50 and arrives in Santa Maria Novella station at around 07.00.

For general rail information see Ⓦ www.raileurope.com. For train travel in Italy see Ⓦ http://trenitalia.it

The monthly *Thomas Cook European Rail Timetable* has up-to-date schedules for European international and national train services. ☎ 01733 416477 (UK); 1 800 322 3834 (USA) Ⓦ www.thomascookpublishing.com

Eurostar (UK) ☎ 0870 518 6186 Ⓦ www.eurostar.com

ENTRY FORMALITIES

EU citizens can remain in Italy for an unlimited period. Visitors from the USA, Canada, Australia and New Zealand do not need visas for stays of up to three months, but South African visitors do require a visa. Everyone must show a valid passport or identity card (EU citizens only) upon entry to Italy.

EU citizens do not have to declare goods imported or exported as long as they are for their personal use and they have arrived from another country within the EU. For non-EU citizens or arrivals from outside the EU, the following import restrictions apply: 400 cigarettes or 200 small cigars or 100 cigars or 500 g of tobacco; 1 litre of spirits or 2 litres of fortified wine; 50 grams of perfume; 10,000 euros in cash.

MONEY

Italy is a member of the European Union and the euro (€) is the official currency. There are seven banknotes: €5, €10, €20, €50, €100, €200 and €500. Coins come in denominations of €1, €2 and 1, 2, 5, 10, 20 and 50 cents.

There are 24-hour ATM machines located outside most banks, as well as at airports and railway stations, accepting Cirrus, Maestro, Visa, Access and MasterCard.

Foreign currencies can be changed at most banks and bureaux de change with a passport or other ID. Traveller's cheques in sterling or dollars can be exchanged in banks, bureaux de change or in some hotels for a commission.

Bureaux de change open out of banking hours, but rates and charges are usually less favourable than those at a bank. The **Thomas Cook Bureau** (ⓐ Lungarno Acciaiuoli 4/8r ① 055 290 278) is open on Sundays and does not charge for currency exchange using Visa and MasterCard.

Visa, MasterCard and usually American Express credit cards are widely accepted in Italy. For lost or stolen credit cards call:
American Express ① 06 72282
American Express Gold Card ① 06 72 900 347
Diners Club ① 800 864 064
Eurocard, **MasterCard**, **Visa** ① 800 15 16 16

HEALTH, SAFETY & CRIME

UK citizens are entitled to the same medical care as Italians on production of a European Health Insurance Card (EHIC). See Ⓦ www.ehic.org.uk for more information on obtaining a card. Non-EU nationals are entitled to free emergency medical care but should take out medical insurance for all other situations.

Dentists are not covered by the EHIC and tend to be more expensive than in Britain.

For a GP you must go to the nearest *Azienda Sanitaria* (Public Health Centre) taking your EHIC with you. Surgeries are usually open 09.00–13.00 & 14.00–19.00 Mon–Fri, and you will be required to pay for your visit. Don't forget to keep proof of payment in order to be reimbursed by your insurance when you arrive home. Medicine and tests may cost extra and the EHIC will not cover repatriation or other costs involved in getting home in an emergency.

If you have to spend time in hospital, you are expected to provide towels and often eating utensils and toilet paper as well. Pharmacies (*farmacie*) can be identified by a green or red cross and staff will advise on non-prescription drugs for minor illnesses. Additional information can be found at:

UK health and travel advice Ⓦ www.fco.gov.uk or Ⓦ www.dh.gov.uk/travellers

US health and travel advice Ⓦ www.cdc.gov/travel or Ⓦ www.healthfinder.gov

World Health Organisation Ⓦ www.who.int/en

Italians tend to drink bottled water although tap water is safe to drink. There are no inoculations necessary for a visit to Italy, although mosquitoes can be annoyingly persistent pests. Carry mosquito repellent, especially if you are leaving the city.

In spring and summer sunburn is a potential risk, so apply sunblock, wear a hat and stay indoors in the middle of the day if you are sensitive.

As in any big city, be aware that street crime is a factor. Pickpockets and moped-riding bag snatchers operate in the tourist areas, on buses and at the railway station. Wear a shoulder bag across your chest and keep it fastened and in sight at all times. Keep wallets out of sight and valuables in your hotel, preferably in a safe.

OPENING HOURS

Opening hours in Florence are both complex and flexible, but the following generalisations apply:

Shops: Small shops open 09.00–19.30 but close 13.00–15.30 for lunch. They generally remain closed on Monday mornings. Larger department stores are open all day. Supermarkets, grocers and markets open earlier and close at 13.00. They reopen around 17.00, except on Wednesdays. All shops generally close on Saturday afternoons in summer and all day on Sunday year round. Some shops close for three weeks in August.

Museums: Museums are often open only in the mornings and some are closed on Mondays. Private museums often open longer hours.

Banks: Bank opening hours are 08.30–13.30 & 15.00–16.30 Mon–Fri. They close on public holidays and work shorter hours the day before.

Pharmacies: Basic pharmacy opening hours are 08.30–13.00 & 16.00–18.00 Mon–Fri, 08.00–13.00 Sat. Duty rosters for out-of-hours pharmacies are posted on the wall next to the door.

TOILETS

Public toilets are a rarity in Florence. If you stop in a bar, it is polite to buy a quick coffee in the bar. There are (paying) public toilets in the underpass by the railway station and in Palazzo Vecchio, Palazzo Pitti, Sant'Ambrogio Market and Piazzale Michelangelo.

CHILDREN

Italy is a very child-oriented country and Florence is no exception. Restaurants welcome children, are smoke-free by law, and some offer children's menus. Parents should be aware of the heat of the sun, even in spring, but beyond that no special health precautions need be taken. Disposable nappies, baby milk and jars of baby food are readily available in supermarkets. Bring any medication with you. Your main problem with bringing children to the city may be that Renaissance paintings and ancient architecture are not their idea of a good day out. There are, however, plenty of places in Florence to keep kids happy.

For an active day out, visit the Giardino di Bóboli (see pages 98–101) with its fountains, grottoes, amphitheatre and summer shows. Or head for the Mondobimbo Inflatables in Piazza della Libertà during June–August, where the kids can work off their energy on big bouncy castles.

⏏ The ornate merry-go-round delights children when it visits every Easter

The Parco delle Cascine, west of the city bordering the river near Ponte della Vittoria Piazzale, is the city's largest park with lots of space to run around and a kiosk hiring inline skates.

For a good hard climb and an ice cream reward at the top head for Piazzale Michelangelo (see page 100). And if they still have some energy left, wear them out climbing the Duomo (see pages 85–6) for some amazing views over the city.

For child-friendly museums, start with La Specola (see page 102), where wax models of dissected bodies offer the 'yuck factor' that many children love. The **Museo de Ragazzi** (Children's Museum ⓐ Palazzo Vecchio, Piazza della Signoria ⓛ 09.30–19.00 daily ⓘ Admission charge) has puppet shows, dressing-up corners, workshops and medieval characters. There are children's workshops in English on some Saturdays. For a more scientific experience, the **Museo Galileo** (ⓐ Piazza dei Giudici 1 ⓦ www.museogalileo.it ⓛ 09.30–13.00 Tues, 09.30–18.00 Wed–Mon ⓘ Admission charge) houses a wonderful array of instruments, including the lens with which Galileo discovered Jupiter's moons. There's also a section on the history of medicine, with a gruesome-looking selection of old surgical instruments. For info on all the above, contact Firenze Musei (ⓣ 055 265 4321).

COMMUNICATION
Internet
Internet access is widespread and there are Internet cafés around the city though ID is required. Many hotels have laptop access points or Wi-Fi for their guests.

Internet Train ⓐ Via dell'Orivolo 40r ⓣ 055 263 8968 ⓛ 10.00–22.00 Mon–Sat, 15.00–21.00 Sun and ⓐ Borgo San Jacopo 30r ⓣ 055 265 7935 ⓛ 10.30–23.00 Mon–Fri, 11.00–23.00 Sat & Sun

Phone

Phone boxes take phonecards (*schede telefoniche*), which can be bought at newsstands or *tabacchi* (tobacconists). Rates are lower after 18.30 and lower still after 22.00. Hotel phone rates are normally astronomical. If you travel to Italy often, it may be worth purchasing an Italian SIM card for your mobile.

TELEPHONING FLORENCE

The area code for Florence is 055, Pisa is 050 and Siena is 0577. When dialling from inside Italy, dial the full number, including the area code. The international dialling code for Italy is 39. To call Florence from abroad, dial either 00 (from the UK), 011 (from the USA) or 0011 (from Australia), followed by the international code (39), followed by the area code (055) and then the local number you require. Note that, unlike in many countries, when telephoning Italy from abroad you do not drop the initial 'o' of the area code.

TELEPHONING ABROAD

From Italy, dial 00, followed by your country code (UK 44; Republic of Ireland 353; USA and Canada 1; Australia 61; New Zealand 64; South Africa 27), followed by the area code (leaving out the first 'o' if there is one) and then the local number you require.

Post

Postal services in Italy are far more reliable these days than in the past. All letters are now sent using *poste priorità* (express post).

Postboxes are red and affixed to building walls. They have two slots – one for letters within the city (*per la Città*) and one for all other destinations and abroad (*Altre Destinazioni*). Stamps can be bought in tobacconists as well as in post offices (*ufficio postale*). Opening hours are approximately 08.15–13.30 Mon–Fri & 08.15–12.30 Sat.

Central post office ⓐ Via Pellicceria 3 ① 055 281 156 ⓒ 08.15–19.00 Mon–Fri, 08.15–12.30 Sat

ADDRESSES

Florence has two sets of numbers for every street. Businesses, shops and restaurants have one set of numbers, recognisable by a red number on the building and written on correspondence and directions with the letter 'r' following the number. Residential addresses are black and have no following letter. There are, however, some variations to this rule.

ELECTRICITY

Electrical current in Italy is 220V AC and plugs are the standard European two round-pin ones. British appliances will need a simple adaptor, easily obtained at any electrical or hardware store in Florence or at the airport. US and other equipment designed for 110v will usually need a transformer (*transformatore di corrente*).

TRAVELLERS WITH DISABILITIES

Recent legislation encouraging improved access facilities means that wheelchair users will find it easier to get around in Florence, although the rules apply only to new buildings. Most modern hotels and museums have ramps and lifts, while the most recently purchased buses have lowering ramps. The few trains with wheelchair access are marked with the standard wheelchair logo. Access to Santa Novella train station is at the east or north side and you can ring in advance for assistance (☏ 055 235 2275). Owners of a disabled driver sticker can drive in pedestrianised areas of the city and there are adequate disabled parking bays around the city. Florence and Pisa airports have disabled toilets, as does Santa Novella station.

A booklet is available from tourist offices with information on the accessibility of various local sights, or you can also check at ⓦ www.comune.fi.it

Useful organisations for advice and information before your travels include:

RADAR The principal UK forum for people with disabilities.
ⓐ 12 City Forum, 250 City Road, London EC1V 8AF ☏ 020 7250 3222
ⓦ www.radar.org.uk

SATH (Society for Accessible Travel & Hospitality) advises US-based travellers with disabilities. ⓐ 347 Fifth Ave, Suite 605, New York, NY 10016 ☏ 212 447 7284 ⓦ www.sath.org

TOURIST INFORMATION

Tourist information offices are located at:
ⓐ Via Cavour 1r ☏ 055 290 832 ⏰ 08.30–18.30 Mon–Sat, 08.30–13.30 Sun
ⓐ Via Manzoni 16 ☏ 055 23320 ⏰ 09.00–13.00 Mon–Fri
ⓐ Piazza della Stazione 4a ☏ 055 212 245 ⏰ 08.30–19.00 Mon–Sat, 08.30–14.00 Sun ⓘ The kiosk inside the Santa Maria Novella station is not a tourist office, although maps are on sale. Take the underpass to the tourist office on the other side of Piazza della Stazione to pick up free maps and information.

ⓐ Borgo Santa Croce 29r ☎ 055 234 0444 ⏱ 09.00–17.00 Mon–Sat, 09.00–14.00 Sun (Apr–Oct); 09.00–17.00 Mon–Sat, 09.00–14.00 Sun (Nov–Mar)

ⓐ Aeroporto Vespucci ☎ 055 315 874, 055 315 878 ⏱ 08.30–20.30 daily

Florence tourist information website Ⓦ www.firenzeturismo.it

ⓔ info@firenzeturismo.it

ENIT, the Italian government's official tourist board, can also send you information packs about Florence and specialist holidays by direct request through their website. Ⓦ www.enit.it

BACKGROUND READING

The Divine Comedy by Dante.

The Prince by Florentine Niccolò Machiavelli is a must-read for the aspiring autocrat.

Pictures from Italy by Charles Dickens.

A Year in Florence by Alexandre Dumas, famed author of *The Three Musketeers*. He wrote the book while visiting in 1840.

The Italian Hours by Henry James and *A Ride on Horseback to Florence through France and Switzerland* by Dalkeith Holmes both give an interesting insight to the city during the 19th century.

Rome, Naples and Florence by Stendhal is a classic text.

The Innocents Abroad by Mark Twain was partly written in Florence.

A Room with a View by E M Forster is set largely in Florence and Tuscany.

The Rise and Fall of the House of Medici by Christopher Hibbert.

Florence: The Biography of a City by Christopher Hibbert.

Emergencies

The following are emergency toll-free numbers:
Ambulance (*Ambulanza*) ❶ 118
Emergency doctor ❶ 118
Fire (*Vigili del Fuoco*) ❶ 115
Police (*Polizia*, English-speaking helpline) ❶ 112

MEDICAL SERVICES

Accident and Emergency (*pronto soccorso*) departments are open 24 hours. The following hospitals have A&E departments:
Santa Maria Nuova ⓐ Piazza Santa Maria Nuova 1 ❶ 055 27581
Ⓝ Bus: C1, C2, 14, 23, 71. This is the most central hospital in Florence and has a 24-hour pharmacy.
Ospedale di Careggi ⓐ Via Pieraccini 17 ❶ 055 794 9644 Ⓝ Bus: 8, 14, 18, 40, 43, 56
Ospedale Meyer Brand-new hospital now part of Ospedale di Careggi ⓐ Via Pieraccini 24 ❶ 055 56621 Ⓝ Bus: 14, 40, 43

There is also a 24-hour pharmacy in the Santa Maria Novella train station.

For further information, contact the tourist office or check the website Ⓦ www.firenzeturismo.it, which offers a comprehensive list of health services for foreigners in Florence.

POLICE

The police are ever present at the major tourist spots. There are three police vans stationed between 08.00 and 19.00 in Piazza della Repubblica, Via dei Calzaiuoli and at the southern entrance to Ponte Vecchio. There are different kinds of policemen (*vigili*, *carabinieri* and *polizia*), but in an emergency any of them will help.

🔺 *The Duomo and ancient city skyline*

▲ *Mounted police patrol Florence's cobbled streets*

In case of theft or other emergency, go directly to the police station in order to make an official declaration. You may need this document in order to make insurance claims. Police stations are at:

LOST PROPERTY
Ufficio Oggetti Trovati (Lost Property Office) ⓐ Via Circondari 17b
ⓣ 055 328 3942 ⓛ 09.00–12.00 Mon, Wed & Fri, 09.00–12.00 & 14.30–16.30 Tues & Thur ⓦ Bus: 23
Santa Maria Novella station ⓐ Platform 16, next to left luggage
ⓣ 055 235 2190 ⓛ 06.00–24.00 daily
   If you lose something in a taxi, phone the taxi company and give the number of the cab.

EMERGENCY PHRASES

Help! | **Fire!** | **Stop!**
Aiuto! | Fuoco! | Fermi!
Ahyootoh! | *Fwohkoh!* | *Fehrmee!*

Call an ambulance/a doctor/the police/the fire service!
Chiami un'ambulanza/un medico/la polizia/i pompieri!
Kyahmee oon ahmboolahntsa/oon mehdeecoh/
lah pohleetseeyah/ee pohmpyehree!

Commissariato di Polizia ⓐ Via Pietrapiana 50r ⓣ 055 203 991
Carabinieri ⓐ Borgo Ognissanti 48 ⓣ 055 24811

EMBASSIES & CONSULATES
Australian Embassy ⓐ Via Antonio Bosio 5, Rome ⓣ 068 52721
ⓦ www.italy.embassy.gov.au
British Consulate ⓐ Lungarno Corsini 2 ⓣ 055 284 133
ⓦ http://ukinitaly.fco.gov.uk/it ⓛ 09.30–12.30 & 14.30–16.30 Mon–Fri
Canadian Embassy ⓐ Via Zara 30, Rome ⓣ 068 54441 ⓦ www.canada.it
Irish Embassy ⓐ Piazza di Campitelli 3, Rome ⓣ 066 979121
New Zealand Embassy ⓐ Via Clitunno 44, Rome ⓣ 066 853 7501
ⓦ www.nzembassy.com
South African Consulate ⓐ Piazza Saltarelli 1 ⓣ 055 281 863
ⓦ www.sudafrica.it
US Consulate ⓐ Lungarno Amerigo Vespucci 38 ⓣ 055 239 8276
ⓦ http://florence.usconsulate.gov ⓛ 09.00–12.30 & 14.00–15.30
Mon–Fri

ACKNOWLEDGEMENTS

The publishers would like to thank the following for supplying their copyright photographs for this book: APT Florence, page 13; Dreamstime.com (Ahaze, page 128; W H Chow, pages 100–101; Cmfotoworks, page 43; Michael Cramer, page 123; Tom Davidson, pages 28–9; Marilu, page 67; Cristina Marsi, page 146; Mtr, page 153; Lorenzi Puricelli, page 57; Rodarena, page 47; Ron Sumners, page 35; Xdrew, page 111); iStockphoto.com (Kelly Borsheim, page 68; Lorenzo Colloreta, page 27; Knud Nielsen, page 17); Pat Levy, pages 19, 38, 45, 60, 84 & 107; Gianluca Moggi, pages 40–41, 91, 94, 114, 119, 131, 133, 140; Timothy Sewter, pages 5 & 139; SXC.hu (Pasi Pitkanen, page 9; Petra Starke, page 154); Elizabeth Tomasetti, page 6; Kathryn Tomasetti, pages 21, 31, 53 & 63; Vratislav Wolf, page 74.

Project editor: Ed Robinson
Layout: Paul Queripel
Proofreaders: Karolin Thomas & Cath Senker

Send your thoughts to
books@thomascook.com

- Found a great bar, club, shop or must-see sight that we don't feature?
- Like to tip us off about any information that needs a little updating?
- Want to tell us what you love about this handy little guidebook and more importantly how we can make it even handier?

Then here's your chance to tell all! Send us ideas, discoveries and recommendations today and then look out for your valuable input in the next edition of this title.

Email the above address (stating the title) or write to: pocket guides Series Editor, Thomas Cook Publishing, PO Box 227, Coningsby Road, Peterborough PE3 8SB, UK.

WHAT'S IN YOUR GUIDEBOOK?

Independent authors Impartial up-to-date information from our travel experts who meticulously source local knowledge.

Experience Thomas Cook's 165 years in the travel industry and guidebook publishing enriches every word with expertise you can trust.

Travel know-how Thomas Cook has thousands of staff working around the globe, all living and breathing travel.

Editors Travel-publishing professionals, pulling everything together to craft a perfect blend of words, pictures, maps and design.

You, the traveller We deliver a practical, no-nonsense approach to information, geared to how you really use it.

Useful phrases

English	Italian	Approx pronunciation

BASICS		
Yes	Sì	*See*
No	No	*Noh*
Please	Per favore	*Pehr fahvohreh*
Thank you	Grazie	*Grahtsyeh*
Hello	Buongiorno/Ciao	*Bwonjohrnoh/Chow*
Goodbye	Arrivederci/Ciao	*Ahreevehderchee/Chow*
Excuse me	Scusi	*Skoozee*
Sorry	Mi dispiace	*Mee deespyahcheh*
That's okay	Va bene	*Vah behneh*
I don't speak Italian	Non parlo italiano	*Non pahrloh eetahlyahnoh*
Do you speak English?	Parla inglese?	*Pahrlah eenglehzeh?*
Good morning	Buongiorno	*Bwonjohrnoh*
Good afternoon	Buon pomeriggio	*Bwon pohmehreejoh*
Good evening	Buona sera	*Bwonah sehrah*
Goodnight	Buona notte	*Bwonah nohteh*
My name is ...	Mi chiamo ...	*Mee kyahmoh ...*

NUMBERS		
One	Uno	*Oonoh*
Two	Due	*Dooeh*
Three	Tre	*Treh*
Four	Quattro	*Kwahttroh*
Five	Cinque	*Cheenkweh*
Six	Sei	*Say*
Seven	Sette	*Sehteh*
Eight	Otto	*Ohtoh*
Nine	Nove	*Nohveh*
Ten	Dieci	*Dyehchee*
Twenty	Venti	*Ventee*
Fifty	Cinquanta	*Cheenkwahntah*
One hundred	Cento	*Chentoh*

SIGNS & NOTICES		
Airport	Aeroporto	*Ahehrohpohrtoh*
Railway station	Stazione ferroviaria	*Stahtsyoneh fehrohveeahreeyah*
Platform	Binario	*Beenahreeyoh*
Smoking/Non-smoking	Fumatori/Non fumatori	*Foomahtohree/non foomahtohree*
Toilets	Bagni	*Bahnyee*
Ladies/Gentlemen	Signore/Signori	*Seenyohreh/Seenyohree*
Subway	Metropolitana	*Mehtrohpohleetahnah*